P9-DSZ-022

On
Teams

HBR's 10 Must Reads series is the definitive collection of ideas and best practices for aspiring and experienced leaders alike. These books offer essential reading selected from the pages of *Harvard Business Review* on topics critical to the success of every manager.

Titles include:

HBR's 10 Must Reads on Change Management
HBR's 10 Must Reads on Collaboration
HBR's 10 Must Reads on Communication
HBR's 10 Must Reads on Innovation
HBR's 10 Must Reads on Leadership
HBR's 10 Must Reads on Making Smart Decisions
HBR's 10 Must Reads on Managing People
HBR's 10 Must Reads on Managing Yourself
HBR's 10 Must Reads on Strategic Marketing
HBR's 10 Must Reads on Strategy
HBR's 10 Must Reads on Teams
HBR's 10 Must Reads: The Essentials

On
Teams

HARVARD BUSINESS REVIEW PRESS
Boston, Massachusetts

Copyright 2013 Harvard Business School Publishing Corporation
All rights reserved
Printed in the United States of America
24 23 22 21 20 19 18 17

The web addresses referenced in this book were live and correct at the time
of book's publication but may be subject to change.

Library of Congress Cataloging-in-Publication Data

HBR's 10 must reads on teams.
     pages cm. — (HBR's 10 must reads series)
  Includes index.
  ISBN 978-1-4221-8987-0 (alk. paper)
  1. Teams in the workplace.   I. Harvard Business Review Press.   II. Title:
HBR's ten must reads on teams.   III. Title: 10 must reads on teams.   IV. Title:
Ten must reads on teams.
  HD66.H394 2013
  658.4'022–dc23   2012046240

The paper used in this publication meets the requirements of the American
National Standard for Permanence of Paper for Publications and Documents in
Libraries and Archives Z39.48-1992.

Contents

On
Teams

The New Science of Building Great Teams

The chemistry of high-performing groups is no longer a mystery. *by Alex "Sandy" Pentland*

IF YOU WERE looking for teams to rig for success, a call center would be a good place to start. The skills required for call center work are easy to identify and hire for. The tasks involved are clear-cut and easy to monitor. Just about every aspect of team performance is easy to measure: number of issues resolved, customer satisfaction, average handling time (AHT, the golden standard of call center efficiency). And the list goes on.

Why, then, did the manager at a major bank's call center have such trouble figuring out why some of his teams got excellent results, while other, seemingly similar, teams struggled? Indeed, none of the metrics that poured in hinted at the reason for the performance gaps. This mystery reinforced his assumption that team building was an art, not a science.

The truth is quite the opposite. At MIT's Human Dynamics Laboratory, we have identified the elusive group dynamics that characterize high-performing teams—those blessed with the energy, creativity, and shared commitment to far surpass other teams. These dynamics are observable, quantifiable, and measurable. And, perhaps most important, teams can be taught how to strengthen them.

Why Do Patterns of Communication Matter So Much?

It seems almost absurd that how we communicate could be so much more important to success than what we communicate.

Yet if we look at our evolutionary history, we can see that language is a relatively recent development and was most likely layered upon older signals that communicated dominance, interest, and emotions among humans. Today these ancient patterns of communication still shape how we make decisions and coordinate work among ourselves.

Consider how early man may have approached problem solving. One can imagine humans sitting around a campfire (as a team) making suggestions, relating observations, and indicating interest or approval with head nods, gestures, or vocal signals. If some people failed to contribute or to signal their level of interest or approval, then the group members had less information and weaker judgment, and so were more likely to go hungry.

Looking for the "It Factor"

When we set out to document the behavior of teams that "click," we noticed we could sense a buzz in a team even if we didn't understand what the members were talking about. That suggested that the key to high performance lay not in the content of a team's discussions but in the manner in which it was communicating. Yet little of the research on team building had focused on communication. Suspecting it might be crucial, we decided to examine it more deeply.

For our studies, we looked across a diverse set of industries to find workplaces that had similar teams with varying performance. Ultimately, our research included innovation teams, post-op wards in hospitals, customer-facing teams in banks, backroom operations teams, and call center teams, among others.

We equipped all the members of those teams with electronic badges that collected data on their individual communication behavior—tone of voice, body language, whom they talked to and how much, and more. With remarkable consistency, the data confirmed that communication indeed plays a critical role in building successful teams. In fact, we've found patterns of communication to be the most

Idea in Brief

Why do some teams consistently deliver high performance while other, seemingly identical teams struggle? Led by Sandy Pentland, researchers at MIT's Human Dynamics Laboratory set out to solve that puzzle. Hoping to decode the "It factor" that made groups click, they equipped teams from a broad variety of projects and industries (comprising 2,500 individuals in total) with wearable electronic sensors that collected data on their social behavior for weeks at a time.

With remarkable consistency, the data showed that the most important predictor of a team's success was its communication patterns. Those patterns were as significant as all other factors—intelligence, personality, talent—combined. In fact, the researchers could foretell which teams would outperform simply by looking at the data on their communication, without even meeting their members.

In this article Pentland shares the secrets of his findings and shows how anyone can engineer a great team. He has identified three key communication dynamics that affect performance: *energy, engagement,* and *exploration.* Drawing from the data, he has precisely quantified the ideal team patterns for each. Even more significant, he has seen that when teams map their own communication behavior over time and then make adjustments that move it closer to the ideal, they can dramatically improve their performance.

important predictor of a team's success. Not only that, but they are as significant as all the other factors—individual intelligence, personality, skill, and the substance of discussions—combined.

Patterns of communication, for example, explained why performance varied so widely among the seemingly identical teams in that bank's call center. Several teams there wore our badges for six weeks. When my fellow researchers (my colleagues at Sociometric Solutions—Taemie Kim, Daniel Olguin, and Ben Waber) and I analyzed the data collected, we found that the best predictors of productivity were a team's energy and engagement outside formal meetings. Together those two factors explained one-third of the variations in dollar productivity among groups.

Drawing on that insight, we advised the center's manager to revise the employees' coffee break schedule so that everyone on a team took a break at the same time. That would allow people more time to socialize with their teammates, away from their workstations. Though the suggestion flew in the face of standard efficiency practices, the manager was baffled and desperate, so he tried it. And it worked: AHT fell by more than 20% among lower-performing teams and decreased by 8% overall at the call center. Now the manager is changing the break schedule at all 10 of the bank's call centers (which employ a total of 25,000 people) and is forecasting $15 million a year in productivity increases. He has also seen employee satisfaction at call centers rise, sometimes by more than 10%.

Any company, no matter how large, has the potential to achieve this same kind of transformation. Firms now can obtain the tools and data they need to accurately dissect and engineer high performance. Building great teams has become a science. Here's how it works.

Overcoming the Limits of Observation

When we sense esprit de corps, that perception doesn't come out of the blue; it's the result of our innate ability to process the hundreds of complex communication cues that we constantly send and receive.

But until recently we had never been able to objectively record such cues as data that we could then mine to understand why teams click. Mere observation simply couldn't capture every nuance of human behavior across an entire team. What we had, then, was only a strong sense of the things—good leadership and followership, palpable shared commitment, a terrific brainstorming session—that made a team greater than the sum of its parts.

Recent advances in wireless and sensor technology, though, have helped us overcome those limitations, allowing us to measure that ineffable "It factor." The badges developed at my lab at MIT are in their seventh version. They generate more than 100 data points a minute and work unobtrusively enough that we're confident we're capturing natural behavior. (We've documented a period of adjustment to the badges: Early on, people appear to be aware of them and act unnaturally, but the effect dissipates, usually within an hour.)

We've deployed them in 21 organizations over the past seven years, measuring the communication patterns of about 2,500 people, sometimes for six weeks at a time.

With the data we've collected, we've mapped the communication behaviors of large numbers of people as they go about their lives, at an unprecedented level of detail. The badges produce "sociometrics," or measures of how people interact—such as what tone of voice they use; whether they face one another; how much they gesture; how much they talk, listen, and interrupt; and even their levels of extroversion and empathy. By comparing data gathered from all the individuals on a team with performance data, we can identify the communication patterns that make for successful teamwork.

Those patterns vary little, regardless of the type of team and its goal—be it a call center team striving for efficiency, an innovation team at a pharmaceutical company looking for new product ideas, or a senior management team hoping to improve its leadership. Productive teams have certain data signatures, and they're so consistent that we can predict a team's success simply by looking at the data—without ever meeting its members.

We've been able to foretell, for example, which teams will win a business plan contest, solely on the basis of data collected from team members wearing badges at a cocktail reception. (See "Defend Your Research: We Can Measure the Power of Charisma," HBR January–February 2010.) We've predicted the financial results that teams making investments would achieve, just on the basis of data collected during their negotiations. We can see in the data when team members will report that they've had a "productive" or "creative" day.

The data also reveal, at a higher level, that successful teams share several defining characteristics:

1. Everyone on the team talks and listens in roughly equal measure, keeping contributions short and sweet.

2. Members face one another, and their conversations and gestures are energetic.

3. Members connect directly with one another—not just with the team leader.

4. Members carry on back-channel or side conversations within the team.

5. Members periodically break, go exploring outside the team, and bring information back.

The data also establish another surprising fact: Individual reasoning and talent contribute far less to team success than one might expect. The best way to build a great team is not to select individuals for their smarts or accomplishments but to learn how they communicate and to shape and guide the team so that it follows successful communication patterns.

The Key Elements of Communication

In our research we identified three aspects of communication that affect team performance. The first is *energy,* which we measure by the number and the nature of exchanges among team members. A single exchange is defined as a comment and some acknowledgment—for example, a "yes" or a nod of the head. Normal conversations are often made up of many of these exchanges, and in a team setting more than one exchange may be going on at a time.

The most valuable form of communication is face-to-face. The next most valuable is by phone or videoconference, but with a caveat: Those technologies become less effective as more people participate in the call or conference. The least valuable forms of communication are e-mail and texting. (We collect data on those kinds of communication without using the badges. Still, the number of face-to-face exchanges alone provides a good rough measure of energy.) The number of exchanges engaged in, weighted for their value by type of communication, gives each team member an energy score, which is averaged with other members' results to create a team score.

Energy levels within a team are not static. For instance, in my research group at MIT, we sometimes have meetings at which I update people on upcoming events, rule changes, and other administrative details. These meetings are invariably low energy. But when someone announces a new discovery in the same group, excitement and energy skyrocket as all the members start talking to one another at once.

The second important dimension of communication is *engagement,* which reflects the distribution of energy among team members. In a simple three-person team, engagement is a function of the average amount of energy between A and B, A and C, and B and C. If all members of a team have relatively equal and reasonably high energy with all other members, engagement is extremely strong. Teams that have clusters of members who engage in high-energy communication while other members do not participate don't perform as well. When we observed teams making investment decisions, for instance, the partially engaged teams made worse (less profitable) decisions than the fully engaged teams. This effect was particularly common in far-flung teams that talked mostly by telephone.

The third critical dimension, *exploration,* involves communication that members engage in outside their team. Exploration essentially is the energy between a team and the other teams it interacts with. Higher-performing teams seek more outside connections, we've found. We've also seen that scoring well on exploration is most important for creative teams, such as those responsible for innovation, which need fresh perspectives.

To measure exploration, we have to deploy badges more widely in an organization. We've done so in many settings, including the MIT Media Lab and a multinational company's marketing department, which comprised several teams dedicated to different functions.

Our data also show that exploration and engagement, while both good, don't easily coexist, because they require that the energy of team members be put to two different uses. Energy is a finite resource. The more that people devote to their own team (engagement), the less they have to use outside their team (exploration), and vice versa.

But they must do both. Successful teams, especially successful creative teams, oscillate between exploration for discovery and engagement for integration of the ideas gathered from outside sources. At the MIT Media Lab, this pattern accounted for almost half of the differences in creative output of research groups. And in one industrial research lab we studied, it distinguished teams with high creativity from those with low creativity with almost 90% accuracy.

Beyond Conventional Wisdom

A skeptic would argue that the points about energy, engagement, and exploration are blindingly obvious. But the data from our research improve on conventional wisdom. They add an unprecedented level of precision to our observations, quantify the key dynamics, and make them measurable to an extraordinary degree.

For example, we now know that 35% of the variation in a team's performance can be accounted for simply by the number of face-to-face exchanges among team members. We know as well that the "right" number of exchanges in a team is as many as dozens per working hour, but that going beyond that ideal number decreases performance. We can also state with certainty that in a typical high-performance team, members are listening or speaking to the whole group only about half the time, and when addressing the whole group, each team member speaks for only his or her fair share of time, using brief, to-the-point statements. The other half of the time members are engaging in one-on-one conversations, which are usually quite short. It may seem illogical that all those side exchanges contribute to better performance, rather than distract a team, but the data prove otherwise.

The data we've collected on the importance of socializing not only build on conventional wisdom but sometimes upend it. Social time turns out to be deeply critical to team performance, often accounting for more than 50% of positive changes in communication patterns, even in a setting as efficiency-focused as a call center.

Without the data there's simply no way to understand which dynamics drive successful teams. The managers of one young software company, for instance, thought they could promote better communication among employees by hosting "beer meets" and other events. But the badge data showed that these events had little or no effect. In contrast, the data revealed that making the tables in the company's lunchroom longer, so that strangers sat together, had a huge impact.

A similarly refined view of exploration has emerged in the data. Using fresh perspectives to improve performance is hardly a surprising idea; it's practically management canon. But our research shows that most companies don't do it the right way. Many organizations we've studied seek outside counsel repeatedly from the same sources and only at certain times (when building a business case, say, or doing a postmortem on a project). The best-performing and most creative teams in our study, however, sought fresh perspectives constantly, from all other groups in (and some outside) the organization.

How to Apply the Data

For management tasks that have long defied objective analysis, like team building, data can now provide a foundation on which to build better individual and team performance. This happens in three steps.

Step 1: Visualization

In raw form the data don't mean much to the teams being measured. An energy score of 0.5 may be good for an individual, for example, but descriptions of team dynamics that rely on statistical output are not particularly user-friendly. However, using the formulas we developed to calculate energy, engagement, and exploration, we can create maps of how a team is doing on those dimensions, visualizations that clearly convey the data and are instantly accessible to anyone. The maps starkly highlight weaknesses that teams may not have recognized. They identify low-energy, unengaged team members who, even in the visualization, look as if they're being ignored. (For examples, see the sidebar "Mapping Teamwork.")

When we spot such people, we dig down into their individual badge data. Are they trying to contribute and being ignored or cut off? Do they cut others off and not listen, thereby discouraging colleagues from seeking their opinions? Do they communicate only with one other team member? Do they face other people in meetings or tend to hide from the group physically? Do they speak loudly enough? Perhaps the leader of a team is too dominant; it may be that she is doing most of the talking at meetings and needs to work on

Mapping Teamwork

CONCERNED ABOUT UNEVEN PERFORMANCE across its branches, a bank in Prague outfitted customer-facing teams with electronic sensors for six weeks. The first two maps below display data collected from one team of nine people over the course of different days, and the third illustrates data collected on interactions between management and all the teams.

By looking at the data, we unearthed a divide between teams at the "Soviet era" branches of the bank and teams at more modern facilities. Interestingly, at the Soviet-era branches, where poor team communication was the rule, communication outside teams was much higher, suggesting that those teams were desperately reaching out for answers to their problems. Teams at the modern facilities showed high energy and less need to explore outside. After seeing initial data, the bank's management published these dashboard displays for all the teams to see and also reorganized the teams so that they contained a mix of members from old and new branches. According to the bank, those measures helped improve the working culture within all the teams.

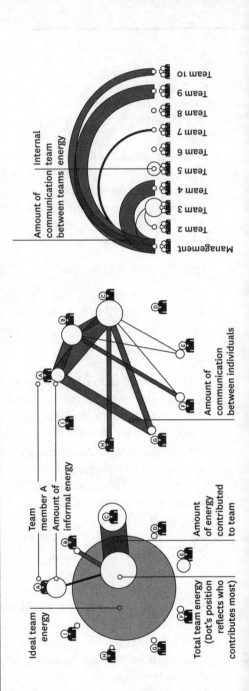

Energy

How team members contribute to a team as a whole

Clearly, these data come from a team at a branch with poor customer service. We can see that A, C, and E give off more informal energy than the rest of the team does. A, B, and C contribute a lot to the team, while the others contribute nothing. The pattern illustrated here is often associated with hierarchical teams in which a boss (C) issues commands while his lieutenants (A and B) reinforce his directions. The three are a "team within a team," and it's likely that the others feel they have no input. Often leaders are shocked and embarrassed to see how much they dominate a team and immediately try to change the pattern. Sharing such a map with the team can make it easier for less energetic individuals to talk about their sense of the team's dysfunction, because data are objective and elevate the discussion beyond attacks or complaints.

Engagement

How team members communicate with one another

This diagram shows that the same team's engagement skews heavily to the same three people (A, B, and C). G is making an effort to reach the decision makers, but the team within the team is where the engagement is. Those three people may be higher up the ladder or simply more extroverted, but that doesn't matter. This pattern is associated with lower performance because the team is not getting ideas or information from many of its members. Leaders can use this map both to assess "invisible" team members (How can they get them more involved? Are they the right people for the project?) and to play the role of a "charismatic connector" by bringing together members who ought to be talking to one another and then helping those members share their thinking with the entire group.

Exploration

How teams communicate with one another

This map shows that management is doing a lot of exploring. Although its internal team energy is relatively low, that is OK. Energy and engagement cannot be high when exploration is, because when you're exploring you have less time to engage with your own team. In a high-functioning organization, however, there would be more exploration among all the teams, and you'd see an arc between, say, Teams 3 and 4, or Teams 5 and 9. A time lapse view of all the teams' exploration would show whether teams were oscillating between communication within their own group (shown by the dots) and exploration with other teams (shown by the arcs). If they're not, it could mean silo busting is needed to encourage proper exploration.

Source: Courtesy of Sociometric Solutions

encouraging others to participate. Energy and engagement maps will make such problems clear. And once we know what they are, we can begin to fix them.

Exploration maps reveal patterns of communication across organizations. They can expose, for instance, whether a department's management is failing to engage with all its teams. Time-lapse views of engagement and exploration will show whether teams are effectively oscillating between those two activities. It's also possible to layer more detail into the visualizations. We can create maps that break out different types of communication among team members, to discover, for example, if teams are falling into counterproductive patterns such as shooting off e-mail when they need more face time. (For an example, see the sidebar "Mapping Communication over Time.")

Mapping Communication over Time

THE MAPS BELOW DEPICT the communication patterns in a German bank's marketing department in the days leading up to and immediately following a major new product launch. The department had teams of four members each in customer service, sales, support, development, and management. Besides collecting data on in-person interactions with sociometric badges, we gathered e-mail data to assess the balance between high-value face-to-face communication and lower-value digital messages.

We did not provide iterative feedback in this project, but if we had, by the end of week one, we would have pointed out three negative trends the group could have corrected: the invisibility of customer service, overreliance on e-mail, and highly uneven communication among groups. If these issues had been addressed, the problems with the product might have surfaced much earlier, and the responses to them would probably have improved.

How to read these maps

Thickness of arcs indicates the amount of communication between groups

Top lines indicate face-to-face communication
Bottom lines indicate communication via e-mail

Day 2: Management is clearly doing most of the communicating.

Day 6: Management by e-mail continues.

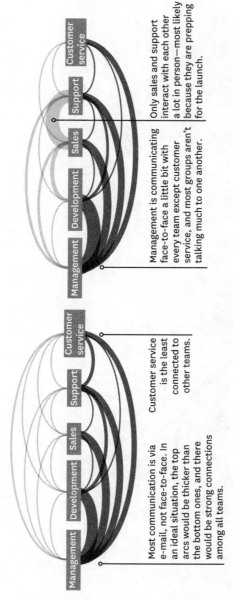

Most communication is via e-mail, not face-to-face. In an ideal situation, the top arcs would be thicker than the bottom ones, and there would be strong connections among all teams.

Customer service is the least connected to other teams.

Management is communicating face-to-face a little bit with every team except customer service, and most groups aren't talking much to one another.

Only sales and support interact with each other a lot in person—most likely because they are prepping for the launch.

(continued)

13

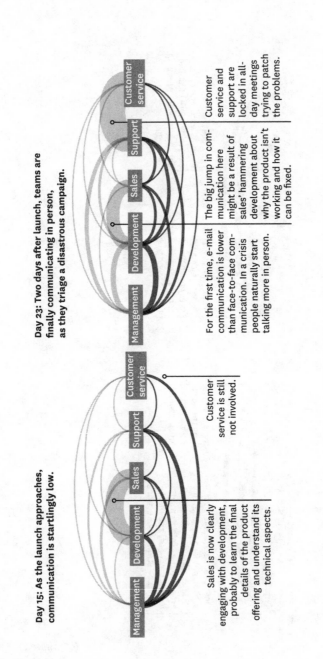

Day 15: As the launch approaches, communication is startlingly low.

Sales is now clearly engaging with development, probably to learn the final details of the product offering and understand its technical aspects.

Customer service is still not involved.

Day 23: Two days after launch, teams are finally communicating in person, as they triage a disastrous campaign.

For the first time, e-mail communication is lower than face-to-face communication. In a crisis people naturally start talking more in person.

The big jump in communication here might be a result of sales' hammering development about why the product isn't working and how it can be fixed.

Customer service and support are locked in all-day meetings trying to patch the problems.

Step 2: Training

With maps of the data in hand, we can help teams improve performance through iterative visual feedback.

Work we did with a multicultural design team composed of both Japanese and American members offers a good example. (Visual data are especially effective at helping far-flung and multilingual groups, which face special communication challenges.) The team's maps (see the sidebar "Mapping communication improvement") showed that its communication was far too uneven. They highlighted that the Japanese members were initially reluctant to speak up, leaving the team both low energy and unengaged.

Mapping Communication Improvement

Our data show that far-flung and mixed-language teams often struggle to gel. Distance plays a role: Electronic communication doesn't create the same energy and engagement that face-to-face communication does. Cultural norms play a role too. Visual feedback on communication patterns can help.

For one week we gathered data on a team composed of Japanese and Americans that were brainstorming a new design together in Japan. Each day the team was shown maps of its communication patterns and given simple guidance about what makes good communication (active but equal participation).

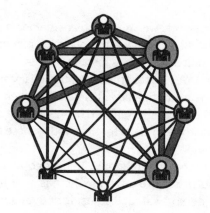

(continued)

Day 1

The two Japanese team members (bottom and lower left) are not engaged, and a team within a team seems to have formed around the member at the top right.

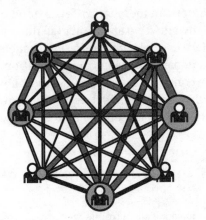

Day 7

The team has improved remarkably. Not only are the Japanese members con-tributing more to energy and engagement (with the one at the bottom becoming a high-energy, highly engaged team member) but some of the Day 1 "dominators" (on the lower right, for example) have distributed their energy better.

Every day for a week, we provided team members a visualization of that day's work, with some light interpretation of what we saw. (Keep in mind that we didn't know the substance of their work, just how they were interacting.) We also told them that the ideal visualization would show members contributing equally and more overall contributions. By day seven, the maps showed, the team's energy and engagement had improved vastly, especially for the two Japanese members, one of whom had become a driving force.

The notion that visual feedback helps people improve quickly shouldn't be surprising to anyone who has ever had a golf swing analyzed on video or watched himself deliver a speech. Now we have the visual tools to likewise improve teamwork through objective analysis.

Step 3: Fine-tuning performance

We have seen that by using visualizations as a training tool, teams can quickly improve their patterns of communication. But does that translate to improved performance? Yes. The third and final step in using the badge data is to map energy and engagement against performance metrics. In the case of the Japanese-American team, for example, we mapped the improved communication patterns against the team's self-reported daily productivity. The closer the patterns came to those of our high-performance ideal, the higher productivity rose.

We've duplicated this result several times over, running similar feedback loops with teams aiming to be more creative and with executive teams looking for more cohesiveness. In every case the self-reporting on effectiveness mapped to the improved patterns of communication.

Through such maps, we often make important discoveries. One of the best examples comes from the bank's call center. For each team there, we mapped energy and engagement against average handling time (AHT), which we indicated with color. (See the sidebar "Mapping Communication Against Performance.") That map clearly showed that the most efficient work was done by high-energy, high-engagement teams. But surprisingly, it also showed that low-energy, low-engagement teams could outperform teams that were unbalanced—teams that had high energy and low engagement, or low energy and high engagement. The maps revealed that the manager needed to keep energy and engagement in balance as he worked to strengthen them.

If a hard metric like AHT isn't available, we can map patterns against subjective measures. We have asked teams to rate their days on a scale of "creativity" or "frustration," for example, and then seen which patterns are associated with highly creative or frustrating days. Teams often describe this feedback as "a revelation."

Mapping Communication Against Performance

VISUALIZATIONS CAN BE USED to compare energy and engagement with established performance metrics. The map below plots the energy and engagement levels of several teams at a bank call center against the center's metric of efficiency, average handling time (AHT).

The expected team efficiency is based on a statistical analysis of actual team AHT scores over six weeks. Blue indicates high efficiency; red low efficiency. High-energy, high-engagement teams are the most efficient, the map shows. But it also indicates that low-energy, low-engagement teams outperform teams that are out of balance, with high energy and low engagement, or low energy and high engagement. This means the call center manager can pull more than one lever to improve performance. **Points Ⓐ and Ⓑ** are equally efficient, for example, but reflect different combinations of energy and engagement.

The manager wanted to raise energy and engagement in lockstep. We suggested instituting a common coffee break for each team at the call center. This increased the number of interactions, especially informal ones, and raised the teams' energy levels. And because all team members took a break at once, interactions were evenly distributed, increasing engagement. When we mapped energy and engagement against AHT afterward, the results were

Successful tactics

The obvious question at this point is, Once I recognize I need to improve energy and engagement, how do I go about doing it? What are the best techniques for moving those measurements?

Simple approaches such as reorganizing office space and seating are effective. So is setting a personal example—when a manager himself actively encourages even participation and conducts more face-to-face communication. Policy changes can improve teams, too. Eschewing Robert's Rules of Order, for example, is a great way to promote change. In some cases, switching out team members and bringing in new blood may be the best way to improve the energy and engagement of the team, though we've found that this is often unnecessary. Most people, given feedback, can learn to interrupt less, say, or to face other people, or to listen more actively. Leaders should use the data to force change within their teams.

clear: Efficiency in the center increased by 8%, on average, and by as much as 20% for the worst-performing teams.

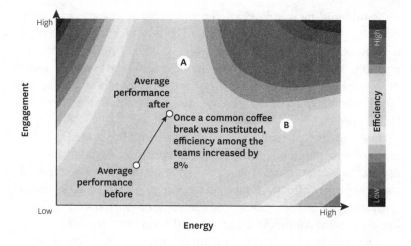

The ideal team player

We can also measure individuals against an ideal. In both productivity-focused and creativity-focused teams, we have discovered the data signature of what we consider the best type of team member. Some might call these individuals "natural leaders." We call them "charismatic connectors." Badge data show that these people circulate actively, engaging people in short, high-energy conversations. They are democratic with their time—communicating with everyone equally and making sure all team members get a chance to contribute. They're not necessarily extroverts, although they feel comfortable approaching other people. They listen as much as or more than they talk and are usually very engaged with whomever they're listening to. We call it "energized but focused listening."

The best team players also connect their teammates with one another and spread ideas around. And they are appropriately exploratory, seeking ideas from outside the group but not at the expense of group engagement. In a study of executives attending an intensive one-week executive education class at MIT, we found that the more of these charismatic connectors a team had, the more successful it was.

Team building is indeed a science, but it's young and evolving. Now that we've established patterns of communication as the single most important thing to measure when gauging the effectiveness of a group, we can begin to refine the data and processes to create more-sophisticated measurements, dig deeper into the analysis, and develop new tools that sharpen our view of team member types and team types.

The sensors that enable this science are evolving as well. As they enter their seventh generation, they're becoming as small and unobtrusive as traditional ID badges, while the amount and types of data they can collect are increasing. We've begun to experiment with apps that present teams and their leaders with real-time feedback on group communications. And the applications for the sensors are expanding beyond the team to include an ever-broader set of situations.

We imagine a company's entire staff wearing badges over an extended period of time, creating "big data" in which we'd find the patterns for everything from team building to leadership to negotiations to performance reviews. We imagine changing the nature of the space we work in, and maybe even the tools we use to communicate, on the basis of the data. We believe we can vastly improve long-distance work and cross-cultural teams, which are so crucial in a global economy, by learning their patterns and adjusting them. We are beginning to create what I call the "God's-eye view" of the organization. But spiritual as that may sound, this view is rooted in evidence and data. It is an amazing view, and it will change how organizations work.

Originally published in April 2012. Reprint R1204C

Why Teams Don't Work

An Interview with J. Richard Hackman. *by Diane Coutu*

OVER THE PAST COUPLE of decades, a cult has grown up around teams. Even in a society as fiercely independent as America, teams are considered almost sacrosanct. The belief that working in teams makes us more creative and productive is so widespread that when faced with a challenging new task, leaders are quick to assume that teams are the best way to get the job done.

Not so fast, says J. Richard Hackman, the Edgar Pierce Professor of Social and Organizational Psychology at Harvard University and a leading expert on teams. Hackman has spent a career exploring—and questioning—the wisdom of teams. To learn from his insights, HBR senior editor Diane Coutu interviewed Hackman in his Harvard office. In the course of their discussion, he revealed just how bad people often are at teamwork. Most of the time, his research shows, team members don't even agree on what the team is supposed to be doing. Getting agreement is the leader's job, and she must be willing to take great personal and professional risks to set the team's direction. And if the leader isn't disciplined about managing who is on the team and how it is set up, the odds are slim that a team will do a good job.

What follows is an edited version of that conversation.

You begin your book Leading Teams *with a pop quiz: When people work together to build a house, will the job probably (a) get done faster, (b) take longer to finish, or (c) not get done?*

That multiple choice question actually appeared on a standard-ized fourth-grade test in Ohio, and the obvious "answer," of course, is supposed to be *a*—the work gets done faster. I love that anecdote because it illustrates how early we're told that teamwork is good. People tend to think that teams are the democratic—and the efficient—way to get things done. I have no question that when you have a team, the possibility exists that it will generate magic, producing something extraordinary, a collective creation of previously unimagined quality or beauty. But don't count on it. Research consistently shows that teams underperform, despite all the extra resources they have. That's because problems with coordination and motivation typically chip away at the benefits of collaboration. And even when you have a strong and cohesive team, it's often in competition with other teams, and that dynamic can also get in the way of real progress. So you have two strikes against you right from the start, which is one reason why having a team is often worse than having no team at all.

You've said that for a team to be successful, it needs to be real. What does that mean?

At the very least, it means that teams have to be bounded. It may seem silly to say this, but if you're going to lead a team, you ought to first make sure that you know who's on it. In our recent book *Senior Leadership Teams,* Ruth Wageman, Debra Nunes, James Burruss, and I collected and analyzed data on more than 120 top teams around the world. Not surprisingly, we found that almost every senior team we studied thought that it had set unambiguous boundaries. Yet when we asked members to describe their team, fewer than 10% agreed about who was on it. And these were teams of senior executives!

Often the CEO is responsible for the fuzziness of team boundaries. Fearful of seeming exclusionary—or, on the other end of the spectrum, determined to put people on the team for purely political reasons—the chief executive frequently creates a dysfunctional team. In truth, putting together a team involves some ruthless decisions about membership; not everyone who wants to be on the team should be included, and some individuals should be forced off.

Idea in Brief

Contrary to conventional wisdom, teams may be your *worst* option for tackling a challenging task. Problems with coordination, motivation, and competition can badly damage team performance.

Even the best leaders can't *make* a team deliver great results. But you can increase the likelihood of success—by setting the right conditions. For example:

- **Designate a "deviant."** Appoint a naysayer who will *challenge satin gro*

challenge the team's desire for too much homogeneity (which stifles creativity).

- **Avoid double digits.** Build teams of no more than nine people. Too many more, and the number of links between members becomes unmanageable.

- **Keep the team together.** Established teams work more effectively than those whose composition changes constantly.

We worked with a large financial services firm where the CFO wasn't allowed on the executive committee because he was clearly a team destroyer. He was disinclined toward teamwork, he was unwilling to work at finding collective solutions, and every team he was on got into trouble. The CEO invited the CFO to stay in his role because he was a truly able executive, but he was not allowed on the senior executive team. Although there were some bruised feelings at first, in the end the CFO was much happier because he didn't have to be in "boring" team meetings, and the team functioned much better without him. The arrangement worked because the CEO communicated extensively with the CFO both before and after every executive committee meeting. And in the CFO's absence, the committee could become a real team.

You also say that a team needs a compelling direction. How does it get one?

There is no one right way to set a direction; the responsibility can fall to the team leader or to someone in the organization outside the team or even to the team itself in the case of partnerships or boards of directors. But however it's done, setting a direction is emotionally demanding because it always involves the exercise of authority, and

Idea in Practice

Additional ideas for getting the best performance from your team.

Be Ruthless About Membership

Putting together a team involves some hard decisions about who will contribute best to accomplishing the team's goals. Not everyone who wants to be on a team should be included, and some individuals should be forced off.

> *Example:* In a large financial services firm, the CFO, a brilliant individual contributor, wasn't allowed on the executive committee because he was clearly disinclined toward teamwork and unwilling to work at finding collective solutions. The team functioned much better without him. The arrangement worked because the CEO communicated extensively with the CFO before and after every executive-committee meeting.

Set a Compelling Direction

Make sure your team members know—and agree on—what they're supposed to be doing together. Unless you articulate a clear direction, different members will likely pursue different agendas.

Embrace Your Own Quirkiness

There's no one right style for leading a team, so don't try to ape someone else's leadership approach. You bring your own strengths and weaknesses to the effort. Exploit what you're great at, and get help in the areas where you're not as competent.

that inevitably arouses angst and ambivalence—for both the person exercising it and the people on the receiving end. Leaders who are emotionally mature are willing and able to move toward anxiety-inspiring situations as they establish a clear, challenging team direction. But in doing so, a leader sometimes encounters resistance so intense that it can place his or her job at risk.

That point was dramatically brought home to me a few years ago by a participant in an executive seminar I was teaching. I'd been talking about how leaders who set direction successfully are unafraid to assume personal responsibility for the mission of the team. I mentioned John F. Kennedy and Martin Luther King, Jr., and I got carried away and said that people who read the New Testament knew that Jesus did not convene little team meetings to decide the

Focus Your Coaching on Group Processes

For your team to reap the benefits of any coaching you provide, you'll need to focus that coaching on enhancing group processes, not on guiding and correcting individual behavior. Also, timing is everything. You'll need to know how to:

- **Run a launch meeting,** so members become oriented to and engaged with their tasks.

- **Help the team conduct midpoint reviews** on what's functioning well—and what isn't. This will enable the team to fine-tune its performance strategy.

- **Take a few minutes when the work is finished** to reflect on what went well—and poorly— and to identify ways team members can make the best use of their knowledge and experience the next time around.

Protect Your Deviant

The deviant you designate will say things that nobody else is willing to articulate—such as "Wait a minute, why are we even doing this at all?" or "We've got to stop and maybe change direction."

These observations can open up creative discussion—but they also raise others' anxiety levels. People may feel compelled to crack down on the deviant and try to get him to stop asking difficult questions— maybe even knock him off the team.

Don't let that happen: If you lose your deviant, your team can become mediocre.

goals of the ministry. One of the executives in the class interrupted me and said, "Are you aware that you've just talked about two assassinations and a crucifixion?"

What are some common fallacies about teams?

People generally think that teams that work together harmoniously are better and more productive than teams that don't. But in a study we conducted on symphonies, we actually found that grumpy orchestras played together slightly better than orchestras in which all the musicians were really quite happy.

That's because the cause-and-effect is the reverse of what most people believe: When we're productive and we've done something good together (and are recognized for it), we feel satisfied, not the other way around. In other words, the mood of the orchestra members after a performance says more about how well they did than the mood beforehand.

Another fallacy is that bigger teams are better than small ones because they have more resources to draw upon. A colleague and I once did some research showing that as a team gets bigger, the number of links that need to be managed among members goes up at an accelerating, almost exponential rate. It's managing the links between members that gets teams into trouble. My rule of thumb is no double digits. In my courses, I never allow teams of more than six students. Big teams usually wind up just wasting everybody's time. That's why having a huge senior leadership team—say, one that includes all the CEO's direct reports—may be worse than having no team at all.

Perhaps the most common misperception about teams, though, is that at some point team members become so comfortable and familiar with one another that they start accepting one another's foibles, and as a result performance falls off. Except for one special type of team, I have not been able to find a shred of evidence to support that premise. There is a study that shows that R&D teams do need an influx of new talent to maintain creativity and freshness— but only at the rate of one person every three to four years. The problem almost always is not that a team gets stale but, rather, that it doesn't have the chance to settle in.

So newness is a liability?

Absolutely. The research confirming that is incontrovertible. Consider crews flying commercial airplanes. The National Transportation Safety Board found that 73% of the incidents in its database occurred on a crew's first day of flying together, before people had the chance to learn through experience how best to operate as a team—and 44% of those took place on a crew's very first flight. Also, a NASA study found that fatigued crews who had a history of working together made about half as many errors as crews composed of rested pilots who had not flown together before.

So why don't airlines stick to the same crews?

Because it isn't efficient from a financial perspective. Financially, you get the most from your capital equipment and labor by treating each airplane and each pilot as an individual unit and then using an algorithm to maximize their utilization. That means that pilots often have to dash up and down the concourses just as passengers do, and sometimes you'll have a pilot who will fly two or three different aircraft with two or three different crews in the course of a single day—which is not so wise if you look at the research. I once asked an operations researcher of an airline to estimate how long it would take, if he and I were assigned to work together on a trip, before we could expect to work together again. He calculated that it would be 5.6 years. Clearly, this is not good from a passenger point of view.

The counterexample, by the way, is the Strategic Air Command, or SAC, which would have delivered nuclear bombs had that become necessary during the Cold War years. SAC teams performed better than any other flight crews that we studied. They trained together as a crew, and they became superb at working together because they had to. When you're working together in real time and there can be no mistakes, then you keep your teams together for years and years rather than constantly change their composition.

If teams need to stay together to achieve the best performance, how do you prevent them from becoming complacent?

This is where what I call a deviant comes in. Every team needs a deviant, someone who can help the team by challenging the tendency to want too much homogeneity, which can stifle creativity and learning. Deviants are the ones who stand back and say, "Well, wait a minute, why are we even doing this at all? What if we looked at the thing backwards or turned it inside out?" That's when people say, "Oh, no, no, no, that's ridiculous," and so the discussion about what's ridiculous comes up. Unlike the CFO I mentioned before, who derailed the team by shutting down discussions, the deviant opens up more ideas, and that gets you a lot more originality. In our research, we've looked carefully at both teams that produced something original and those that were merely average, where nothing really sparkled. It turned out that the teams with deviants outperformed teams without them. In many cases, deviant thinking is a source of great innovation.

I would add, though, that often the deviant veers from the norm at great personal cost. Deviants are the individuals who are willing to say the thing that nobody else is willing to articulate. The deviant raises people's level of anxiety, which is a brave thing to do. When the boat is floating with the current, it really is extraordinarily courageous for somebody to stand up and say, "We've got to pause and probably change direction." Nobody on the team wants to hear that, which is precisely why many team leaders crack down on deviants and try to get them to stop asking difficult questions, maybe even knock them off the team. And yet it's when you lose the deviant that the team can become mediocre.

What makes a team effective, and how can a team's leader make it perform better?

A good team will satisfy its internal or external clients, become stronger as a unit as time passes, and foster the learning and growth of its individual members. But even the best leader on the planet can't make a team do well. All anyone can do is increase the likelihood that a team will be great by putting into place five conditions. (See the sidebar "How to Build a Team.") And the leader still will have no guarantees that she will create a magical team. Teams create their own realities and control their own destinies to a greater extent, and far sooner in their existence, than most team leaders realize.

In 1990 I edited a collection of essays by colleagues who had studied teams performing diverse tasks in 27 organizations—everything from a children's theater company to a mental-health-treatment team to a beer-sales-and-delivery team. In those studies, we found that the things that happen the first time a group meets strongly affect how the group operates throughout its entire life. Indeed, the first few minutes of the start of any social system are the most important because they establish not only where the group is going but also what the relationship will be between the team leader and the group, and what basic norms of conduct will be expected and enforced.

How to Build a Team

IN HIS BOOK *LEADING TEAMS*, J. Richard Hackman sets out five basic conditions that leaders of companies and other organizations must fulfill in order to create and maintain effective teams:

1. **Teams must be real.** People have to know who is on the team and who is not. It's the leader's job to make that clear.

2. **Teams need a compelling direction.** Members need to know, and agree on, what they're supposed to be doing together. Unless a leader articulates a clear direction, there is a real risk that different members will pursue different agendas.

3. **Teams need enabling structures.** Teams that have poorly designed tasks, the wrong number or mix of members, or fuzzy and unenforced norms of conduct invariably get into trouble.

4. **Teams need a supportive organization.** The organizational context—including the reward system, the human resource system, and the information system—must facilitate teamwork.

5. **Teams need expert coaching.** Most executive coaches focus on individual performance, which does not significantly improve teamwork. Teams need coaching as a group in team processes—especially at the beginning, midpoint, and end of a team project.

I once asked Christopher Hogwood, the distinguished conductor for many years of the Handel and Haydn Society in Boston, how important the first rehearsal was when he served as an orchestra's guest conductor. "What do you mean, the first *rehearsal?*" he asked. "All I have is the first few minutes." He went on to explain that there's nothing he pays greater attention to than the way he starts the first rehearsal. That's because he knows that the orchestra members will make a very quick assessment about whether or not they're going to make great music together, or whether he is just going to get in their way.

I do think there is one thing leaders such as Hogwood and others can do to improve the chances that a team will become something special, and that is to embrace their own quirkiness. You shouldn't try to lead like Jeff Bezos, because you are not Jeff Bezos. Each leader brings to the task his or her own strengths and weaknesses.

Off and Running: Barack Obama Jump-Starts His Team

by Michael Beschloss

IF THE LAUNCH OF a team is as critical as Professor J. Richard Hackman says, then Barack Obama has done pretty well. He appointed his administration's top officials much faster than most presidents do. Given the monumental crises that faced him the moment he was elected, he had to move quickly. The downside of speed was that some of his choices didn't work out—notably Bill Richardson and Tom Daschle. Obama has certainly brought onto his team people of strong temperaments and contrasting views, starting with Hillary Clinton at the State Department and Jim Jones at the National Security Council. This suggests that we have a president who is unusually sure of his own ability to absorb differing opinions. Appointing people like Clinton also shows his eagerness to harness the talent of his former opponents. Compare that with the record of George W. Bush; his people told many job seekers who had supported John McCain in the 2000 Republican primaries, "Sorry, you backed the wrong horse!"

Of course, Obama is taking a risk by hiring so many strong and contentious personalities. He will inevitably have to spend a lot of time and energy serving as referee. This is what happened with Franklin Roosevelt, who also brought strong-minded figures into his government. One difference with Obama, however, is that FDR temperamentally loved the infighting. He liked to pit people against one another, believing that competition evoked the best performance from everyone. At times FDR actually enjoyed making his underlings suffer. I don't think Obama does.

Most presidents prefer a happy ship, and in some cases their definition of loyalty includes not rocking the boat on major administration programs. Richard Nixon fired his interior secretary, Walter Hickel, for opposing his Vietnam War policies. There was a dissenter (what Hackman calls a deviant) on Lyndon Johnson's team—Undersecretary of State George Ball, who strongly opposed the Vietnam War. Johnson would cite Ball when people complained that he surrounded himself with yes-men, but in fact Ball had little influence when LBJ met with top officials on Vietnam. Everyone in the group knew that Johnson didn't take Ball's antiwar arguments very seriously. If you really want dissenting views, better to use the Roosevelt-Obama model, where they can come from almost any member of the team—and not just from one designated rabble-rouser.

The reappointment of Bush's defense secretary, Robert Gates, also reveals Obama's self-confidence. He's clearly willing to concede that there are things he doesn't know, so he appointed someone with more than three decades of national security experience. This decision has the historical echo of John Kennedy's near-reappointment in 1961 of Dwight Eisenhower's defense secretary, who coincidentally was named Thomas Gates. Like Obama, Kennedy was a young president with little national security background and thought it might reassure people to have the previous defense secretary stay on at the Pentagon. Like Obama, JFK also suspected that a number of things might go wrong with national security during his first year as president. He felt that Americans might be less likely to blame the Democratic president if a Republican secretary of defense was there at his side. In the end Kennedy did not have the stomach for the risk of keeping a Republican appointee at the Pentagon. Obama did.

Obama's first months in office prove the importance of having a president who can convey his view of the country and the world and why he thinks his plans will work. One of Hillary Clinton's biggest criticisms a year ago was that Obama gave great speeches but that it didn't have all that much to do with being a strong president. Obama argued that it did, and he was right. Like Roosevelt's addresses in 1933 and Reagan's in 1981, his public utterances—especially his speech to Congress in February—have done a lot to gain acceptance for his programs from skeptical Americans. However jaded they may be about government, Americans—even those who didn't vote for him—are still inclined to turn to their president to explain foreign and domestic crises. Imagine how much more anxious they might feel now if Obama did not do this so effectively. Unfortunately for us all, it's likely that he'll have to call more on that skill as the crisis mounts in the months ahead.

Michael Beschloss has written nine books about presidential leadership, most recently *Presidential Courage* (Simon & Schuster, 2007).

Exploit the daylights out of the stuff you're great at, and get help in the areas where you're not so good. Don't try to ape any leadership model or team, because there's no one right style for leading a team. There are many different ways to create the conditions for effectiveness, sustain them, and help teams take full advantage of them. The best team leaders are like jazz players, improvising constantly as they go along.

How good are companies at providing a supportive context for teams?

Perversely, the organizations with the best human resource departments often do things that are completely at odds with good team behavior. That's because HR departments tend to put in place systems that are really good at guiding, directing, and correcting individual behavior. Take a personnel system that has been honed by industrial psychologists to identify the skills of a particular job and test individual employees on those skills. In such a system, the HR department will set up training to develop the "right" people in the "right" way. The problem is this is all about the individual. This single-minded focus on the individual employee is one of the main reasons that teams don't do as well as they might in organizations with strong HR departments. Just look at our research on senior executive teams. We found that coaching individual team members did not do all that much to help executive teams perform better.

For the team to reap the benefits of coaching, it must focus on group processes. And timing is everything. The team leader needs to know how to run a launch meeting, so that members become oriented to and engaged with their tasks; how to help the team review at the midpoint what's functioning well—and what isn't—which can correct the team's performance strategy; and how to take a few minutes when the work is finished to reflect on what went well or poorly, which can help members make better use of their knowledge and experience the next time around. Team coaching is about fostering better teamwork on the task, not about enhancing members' social interactions or interpersonal relationships.

There's a lot of talk about virtual teams these days. Can they work, or are they falling victim to what Jo Freeman once called the "tyranny of structurelessness"?

Virtual teams have really come into their own in the past decade, but I don't believe they differ fundamentally from traditional teams. There was a fantasy in the beginning that everyone would be swarming around on the internet, that the wisdom of crowds would automatically prevail, and that structureless groups would come up with new and profound things that face-to-face groups could never have generated. But nirvana never materialized; virtual teams need the basic conditions for effectiveness to be in place just as much as face-to-face teams, if not more so. That said, we are seeing that we can make do with much less face-to-face contact than we ever thought possible. Today's technology, for example, lets you have a chat window open during a web conference so you can type in the word "hand" to signal that you want to talk next. People don't need to see your face to know that you want to speak up. But even well-structured virtual teams need to have a launch meeting with everyone present, a midpoint check-in that's face-to-face, and a live debriefing. I don't think for a minute that we're going to have effective online teams if we don't know who's on the team or what the main work of the team really is, and so far that's still a problem with virtual teams.

Given the difficulty of making teams work, should we be rethinking their importance in organizations?

Perhaps. Many people act as if being a team player is the ultimate measure of one's worth, which it clearly is not. There are many things individuals can do better on their own, and they should not be penalized for it. Go back for a moment to that fourth-grade question about working together to build a house. The answer probably is that teamwork really does take longer or that the house may not get built at all. There are many cases where collaboration, particularly in truly creative endeavors, is a hindrance rather than a help. The challenge for a leader, then, is to find a balance between individual autonomy and collective action. Either extreme is bad, though we are generally more aware of the downside of individualism in organizations, and we forget that teams can be just as destructive by being so strong and controlling that individual voices and contributions and learning are lost.

In one management team we studied, for example, being a team player was so strongly valued that individuals self-censored their contributions for fear of disrupting team harmony. The team, in a spirit of cooperation and goodwill, embarked on a course of action that was bound to fail—for reasons that some members sensed but did not mention as the plans were being laid. One wonders if the crisis in the financial world today would be quite so catastrophic if more people had spoken out in their team meetings about what they knew to be wrongful practices. But again that brings us back to the hazards of courage. You'd like to think that people who do the courageous right thing and speak out will get their reward on earth as well as in heaven. But you don't always get your reward here on earth. While it's true that not being on a team can put your career on hold, being a real and committed team player—whether as a team leader, a deviant, or just a regular member who speaks the truth—can be dangerous business indeed.

Originally published in May 2009. Reprint R0905H

The Discipline of Teams

by Jon R. Katzenbach and Douglas K. Smith

EARLY IN THE 1980S, Bill Greenwood and a small band of rebel rail-roaders took on most of the top management of Burlington Northern and created a multibillion-dollar business in "piggybacking" rail services despite widespread resistance, even resentment, within the company. The Medical Products Group at Hewlett-Packard owes most of its leading performance to the remarkable efforts of Dean Morton, Lew Platt, Ben Holmes, Dick Alberding, and a handful of their colleagues who revitalized a health care business that most others had written off. At Knight Ridder, Jim Batten's "customer obsession" vision took root at the *Tallahassee Democrat* when 14 frontline enthusiasts turned a charter to eliminate errors into a mission of major change and took the entire paper along with them.

Such are the stories and the work of teams—real teams that perform, not amorphous groups that we call teams because we think that the label is motivating and energizing. The difference between teams that perform and other groups that don't is a subject to which most of us pay far too little attention. Part of the problem is that "team" is a word and concept so familiar to everyone. (See the exhibit "Not all groups are teams: How to tell the difference.")

Or at least that's what we thought when we set out to do research for our book *The Wisdom of Teams* (HarperBusiness, 1993). We wanted to discover what differentiates various levels of team

---

Not all groups are teams: How to tell the difference

Working group	Team
• Strong, clearly focused leader	• Shared leadership roles
• Individual accountability	• Individual and mutual accountability
• The group's purpose is the same as the broader organizational mission	• Specific team purpose that the team itself delivers
• Individual work products	• Collective work products
• Runs efficient meetings	• Encourages open-ended discussion and active problem-solving meetings
• Measures its effectiveness indirectly by its influence on others (such as financial performance of the business)	• Measures performance directly by assessing collective work products
• Discusses, decides, and delegates	• Discusses, decides, and does real work together

---

performance, where and how teams work best, and what top management can do to enhance their effectiveness. We talked with hundreds of people on more than 50 different teams in 30 companies and beyond, from Motorola and Hewlett-Packard to Operation Desert Storm and the Girl Scouts.

We found that there is a basic discipline that makes teams work. We also found that teams and good performance are inseparable: You cannot have one without the other. But people use the word "team" so loosely that it gets in the way of learning and applying the discipline that leads to good performance. For managers to make better decisions about whether, when, or how to encourage and use teams, it is important to be more precise about what a team is and what it isn't.

Most executives advocate teamwork. And they should. Teamwork represents a set of values that encourage listening and responding constructively to views expressed by others, giving others the benefit of the doubt, providing support, and recognizing the interests and achievements of others. Such values help teams perform, and they also promote individual performance as well as the performance of

Idea in Brief

The word *team* gets bandied about so loosely that many managers are oblivious to its real meaning—or its true potential. With a run-of-the-mill working group, performance is a function of what the members do as individuals. A team's performance, by contrast, calls for both individual and mutual accountability.

Though it may not seem like anything special, mutual accountability can lead to astonishing results. It enables a team to achieve performance levels that are far greater than the individual bests of the team's members. To achieve these benefits, team members must do more than listen, respond constructively, and provide support to one another. In addition to sharing these team-building values, they must share an essential *discipline*.

an entire organization. But teamwork values by themselves are not exclusive to teams, nor are they enough to ensure team performance. (See the sidebar "Building Team Performance.")

Nor is a team just any group working together. Committees, councils, and task forces are not necessarily teams. Groups do not become teams simply because that is what someone calls them. The entire workforce of any large and complex organization is *never* a team, but think about how often that platitude is offered up.

To understand how teams deliver extra performance, we must distinguish between teams and other forms of working groups. That distinction turns on performance results. A working group's performance is a function of what its members do as individuals. A team's performance includes both individual results and what we call "collective work products." A collective work product is what two or more members must work on together, such as interviews, surveys, or experiments. Whatever it is, a collective work product reflects the joint, real contribution of team members.

Working groups are both prevalent and effective in large organizations where individual accountability is most important. The best working groups come together to share information, perspectives, and insights; to make decisions that help each person do his or her job better; and to reinforce individual performance standards.

Idea in Practice

A team's essential discipline comprises five characteristics:

1. **A meaningful common purpose that the team has helped shape.** Most teams are responding to an initial mandate from outside the team. But to be successful, the team must "own" this purpose, develop its own spin on it.

2. **Specific performance goals that flow from the common purpose.** For example, getting a new product to market in less than half the normal time. Compelling goals inspire and challenge a team, give it a sense of urgency. They also have a leveling effect, requiring members to focus on the collective effort necessary rather than any differences in title or status.

3. **A mix of complementary skills.** These include technical or functional expertise, problem-solving and decision-making skills, and interpersonal skills. Successful teams rarely have all the needed skills at the outset— they develop them as they learn what the challenge requires.

4. **A strong commitment to how the work gets done.** Teams must agree on who will do what jobs, how schedules will be established and honored, and how decisions will be made and modified. On a genuine team, each member does equivalent amounts of real work; all members, the leader included, contribute in concrete ways to the team's collective work-products.

But the focus is always on individual goals and accountabilities. Working-group members don't take responsibility for results other than their own. Nor do they try to develop incremental performance contributions requiring the combined work of two or more members.

Teams differ fundamentally from working groups because they require both individual and mutual accountability. Teams rely on more than group discussion, debate, and decision, on more than sharing information and best-practice performance standards. Teams produce discrete work products through the joint contributions of their members. This is what makes possible performance levels greater than the sum of all the individual bests of team members. Simply stated, a team is more than the sum of its parts.

5. **Mutual accountability.** Trust and commitment cannot be coerced. The process of agreeing upon appropriate goals serves as the crucible in which members forge their accountability to each other—not just to the leader.

Once the essential discipline has been established, a team is free to concentrate on the critical challenges it faces:

- For a team whose purpose is to make recommendations, that means making a fast and constructive start and providing a clean handoff to those who will implement the recommendations.

- For a team that makes or does things, it's keeping the specific performance goals in sharp focus.

- For a team that runs things, the primary task is distinguishing the challenges that require a real team approach from those that don't.

If a task doesn't demand joint work-products, a working group can be the more effective option. Team opportunities are usually those in which hierarchy or organizational boundaries inhibit the skills and perspectives needed for optimal results. Little wonder, then, that teams have become the primary units of productivity in high-performance organizations.

The first step in developing a disciplined approach to team management is to think about teams as discrete units of performance and not just as positive sets of values. Having observed and worked with scores of teams in action, both successes and failures, we offer the following. Think of it as a working definition or, better still, an essential discipline that real teams share: *A team is a small number of people with complementary skills who are committed to a common purpose, set of performance goals, and approach for which they hold themselves mutually accountable.*

The essence of a team is common commitment. Without it, groups perform as individuals; with it, they become a powerful unit of collective performance. This kind of commitment requires a purpose in which team members can believe. Whether the purpose is to

Building Team Performance

ALTHOUGH THERE IS NO guaranteed how-to recipe for building team perform-ance, we observed a number of approaches shared by many successful teams.

Establish urgency, demanding performance standards, and direction. All team members need to believe the team has urgent and worthwhile purposes, and they want to know what the expectations are. Indeed, the more urgent and meaningful the rationale, the more likely it is that the team will live up to its performance potential, as was the case for a customer-service team that was told that further growth for the entire company would be impossible without major improvements in that area. Teams work best in a compelling context. That is why companies with strong performance ethics usually form teams readily.

Select members for skill and skill potential, not personality. No team succeeds without all the skills needed to meet its purpose and performance goals. Yet most teams figure out the skills they will need after they are formed. The wise manager will choose people for their existing skills and their potential to improve existing skills and learn new ones.

Pay particular attention to first meetings and actions. Initial impressions al-ways mean a great deal. When potential teams first gather, everyone monitors the signals given by others to confirm, suspend, or dispel assumptions and concerns. They pay particular attention to those in authority: the team leader and any executives who set up, oversee, or otherwise influence the team. And, as always, what such leaders do is more important than what they say. If a sen-ior executive leaves the team kickoff to take a phone call ten minutes after the session has begun and he never returns, people get the message.

Set some clear rules of behavior. All effective teams develop rules of conduct at the outset to help them achieve their purpose and performance goals. The most critical initial rules pertain to attendance (for example, "no interruptions to take phone calls"), discussion ("no sacred cows"), confidentiality ("the only things to leave this room are what we agree on"), analytic approach ("facts are friendly"), end-product orientation ("everyone gets assignments and does them"), constructive confrontation ("no finger pointing"), and, often the most important, contributions ("everyone does real work").

"transform the contributions of suppliers into the satisfaction of customers," to "make our company one we can be proud of again," or to "prove that all children can learn," credible team purposes have an element related to winning, being first, revolutionizing, or being on the cutting edge.

Set and seize upon a few immediate performance-oriented tasks and goals. Most effective teams trace their advancement to key performance-oriented events. Such events can be set in motion by immediately establishing a few challenging goals that can be reached early on. There is no such thing as a real team without performance results, so the sooner such results occur, the sooner the team congeals.

Challenge the group regularly with fresh facts and information. New information causes a team to redefine and enrich its understanding of the performance challenge, thereby helping the team shape a common purpose, set clearer goals, and improve its common approach. A plant quality improvement team knew the cost of poor quality was high, but it wasn't until they researched the different types of defects and put a price tag on each one that they knew where to go next. Conversely, teams err when they assume that all the information needed exists in the collective experience and knowledge of their members.

Spend lots of time together. Common sense tells us that team members must spend a lot of time together, scheduled and unscheduled, especially in the beginning. Indeed, creative insights as well as personal bonding require impromptu and casual interactions just as much as analyzing spreadsheets and interviewing customers. Busy executives and managers too often intentionally minimize the time they spend together. The successful teams we've observed all gave themselves the time to learn to be a team. This time need not always be spent together physically; electronic, fax, and phone time can also count as time spent together.

Exploit the power of positive feedback, recognition, and reward. Positive reinforcement works as well in a team context as elsewhere. Giving out "gold stars" helps shape new behaviors critical to team performance. If people in the group, for example, are alert to a shy person's initial efforts to speak up and contribute, they can give the honest positive reinforcement that encourages continued contributions. There are many ways to recognize and reward team performance beyond direct compensation, from having a senior executive speak directly to the team about the urgency of its mission to using awards to recognize contributions. Ultimately, however, the satisfaction shared by a team in its own performance becomes the most cherished reward.

Teams develop direction, momentum, and commitment by working to shape a meaningful purpose. Building ownership and commitment to team purpose, however, is not incompatible with taking initial direction from outside the team. The often-asserted assumption that a team cannot "own" its purpose unless management leaves it alone actually confuses more potential teams than it helps. In fact, it is the exceptional case—for example, entrepreneurial situations—when a team creates a purpose entirely on its own.

Most successful teams shape their purposes in response to a demand or opportunity put in their path, usually by higher management. This helps teams get started by broadly framing the company's performance expectation. Management is responsible for clarifying the charter, rationale, and performance challenge for the team, but management must also leave enough flexibility for the team to develop commitment around its own spin on that purpose, set of specific goals, timing, and approach.

The best teams invest a tremendous amount of time and effort exploring, shaping, and agreeing on a purpose that belongs to them both collectively and individually. This "purposing" activity continues throughout the life of the team. By contrast, failed teams rarely develop a common purpose. For whatever reason—an insufficient focus on performance, lack of effort, poor leadership—they do not coalesce around a challenging aspiration.

The best teams also translate their common purpose into specific performance goals, such as reducing the reject rate from suppliers by 50% or increasing the math scores of graduates from 40% to 95%. Indeed, if a team fails to establish specific performance goals or if those goals do not relate directly to the team's overall purpose, team members become confused, pull apart, and revert to mediocre performance. By contrast, when purposes and goals build on one another and are combined with team commitment, they become a powerful engine of performance.

Transforming broad directives into specific and measurable performance goals is the surest first step for a team trying to shape a purpose meaningful to its members. Specific goals, such as getting a new product to market in less than half the normal time, responding to all customers within 24 hours, or achieving a zero-defect rate while simultaneously cutting costs by 40%, all provide firm footholds for teams. There are several reasons:

- Specific team-performance goals help define a set of work products that are different both from an organization-wide mission and from individual job objectives. As a result, such work products require the collective effort of team members to make something specific happen that, in and of itself, adds real value to results. By contrast, simply gathering from time to time to make decisions will not sustain team performance.

- The specificity of performance objectives facilitates clear communication and constructive conflict within the team. When a plant-level team, for example, sets a goal of reducing average machine changeover time to two hours, the clarity of the goal forces the team to concentrate on what it would take either to achieve or to reconsider the goal. When such goals are clear, discussions can focus on how to pursue them or whether to change them; when goals are ambiguous or nonexistent, such discussions are much less productive.

- The attainability of specific goals helps teams maintain their focus on getting results. A product-development team at Eli Lilly's Peripheral Systems Division set definite yardsticks for the market introduction of an ultrasonic probe to help doctors locate deep veins and arteries. The probe had to have an audible signal through a specified depth of tissue, be capable of being manufactured at a rate of 100 per day, and have a unit cost less than a preestablished amount. Because the team could measure its progress against each of these specific objectives, the team knew throughout the development process where it stood. Either it had achieved its goals or not.

- As Outward Bound and other team-building programs illustrate, specific objectives have a leveling effect conducive to team behavior. When a small group of people challenge themselves to get over a wall or to reduce cycle time by 50%, their respective titles, perks, and other stripes fade into the background. The teams that succeed evaluate what and how each individual can best contribute to the team's goal and, more important, do so in terms of the performance objective itself rather than a person's status or personality.

- Specific goals allow a team to achieve small wins as it pursues its broader purpose. These small wins are invaluable to building commitment and overcoming the inevitable obstacles that get in the way of a long-term purpose. For example, the Knight Ridder team mentioned at the outset turned a narrow goal to eliminate errors into a compelling customer service purpose.

- Performance goals are compelling. They are symbols of accomplishment that motivate and energize. They challenge the people on a team to commit themselves, as a team, to make a difference. Drama, urgency, and a healthy fear of failure combine to drive teams that have their collective eye on an attainable, but challenging, goal. Nobody but the team can make it happen. It's their challenge.

The combination of purpose and specific goals is essential to performance. Each depends on the other to remain relevant and vital. Clear performance goals help a team keep track of progress and hold itself accountable; the broader, even nobler, aspirations in a team's purpose supply both meaning and emotional energy.

Virtually all effective teams we have met, read, or heard about, or been members of have ranged between two and 25 people. For example, the Burlington Northern piggybacking team had seven members, and the Knight Ridder newspaper team had 14. The majority of them have numbered less than ten. Small size is admittedly more of a pragmatic guide than an absolute necessity for success. A large number of people, say 50 or more, can theoretically become a team. But groups of such size are more likely to break into subteams rather than function as a single unit.

Why? Large numbers of people have trouble interacting constructively as a group, much less doing real work together. Ten people are far more likely than 50 to work through their individual, functional, and hierarchical differences toward a common plan and to hold themselves jointly accountable for the results.

Large groups also face logistical issues, such as finding enough physical space and time to meet. And they confront more complex constraints, like crowd or herd behaviors, which prevent the intense sharing of viewpoints needed to build a team. As a result, when they try to develop a common purpose, they usually produce only superficial "missions" and well-meaning intentions that cannot be translated into concrete objectives. They tend fairly quickly to reach a point when meetings become a chore, a clear sign that most of the people in the group are uncertain why they have gathered, beyond some notion of getting along better. Anyone who has been through one of these exercises understands how frustrating it can be. This kind of failure tends to foster cynicism, which gets in the way of future team efforts.

In addition to finding the right size, teams must develop the right mix of skills; that is, each of the complementary skills necessary to do the team's job. As obvious as it sounds, it is a common failing in potential teams. Skill requirements fall into three fairly self-evident categories.

Technical or Functional Expertise

It would make little sense for a group of doctors to litigate an employment discrimination case in a court of law. Yet teams of doctors and lawyers often try medical malpractice or personal injury cases. Similarly, product development groups that include only marketers or engineers are less likely to succeed than those with the complementary skills of both.

Problem-Solving and Decision-Making Skills

Teams must be able to identify the problems and opportunities they face, evaluate the options they have for moving forward, and then make necessary trade-offs and decisions about how to proceed. Most teams need some members with these skills to begin with, although many will develop them best on the job.

Interpersonal Skills

Common understanding and purpose cannot arise without effective communication and constructive conflict, which in turn depend on interpersonal skills. These skills include risk taking, helpful criticism, objectivity, active listening, giving the benefit of the doubt, and recognizing the interests and achievements of others.

Obviously, a team cannot get started without some minimum complement of skills, especially technical and functional ones. Still, think about how often you've been part of a team whose members were chosen primarily on the basis of personal compatibility or formal position in the organization, and in which the skill mix of its members wasn't given much thought.

It is equally common to overemphasize skills in team selection. Yet in all the successful teams we've encountered, not one had all the needed skills at the outset. The Burlington Northern team, for example, initially had no members who were skilled marketers despite the fact that their performance challenge was a marketing one. In fact, we discovered that teams are powerful vehicles for developing the skills needed to meet the team's performance challenge. Accordingly, team member selection ought to ride as much on skill potential as on skills already proven.

Effective teams develop strong commitment to a common approach; that is, to how they will work together to accomplish their purpose. Team members must agree on who will do particular jobs, how schedules will be set and adhered to, what skills need to be developed, how continuing membership in the team is to be earned, and how the group will make and modify decisions. This element of commitment is as important to team performance as the team's commitment to its purpose and goals.

Agreeing on the specifics of work and how they fit together to integrate individual skills and advance team performance lies at the heart of shaping a common approach. It is perhaps self-evident that an approach that delegates all the real work to a few members (or staff outsiders) and thus relies on reviews and meetings for its only "work together" aspects, cannot sustain a real team. Every member of a successful team does equivalent amounts of real work; all members, including the team leader, contribute in concrete ways to the team's work product. This is a very important element of the emotional logic that drives team performance.

When individuals approach a team situation, especially in a business setting, each has preexisting job assignments as well as strengths and weaknesses reflecting a variety of talents, backgrounds, personalities, and prejudices. Only through the mutual discovery and understanding of how to apply all its human resources to a common purpose can a team develop and agree on the best approach to achieve its goals. At the heart of such long and, at times, difficult interactions lies a commitment-building process in which the team candidly explores who is best suited to each task as well as how individual roles will come together. In effect, the team establishes a social contract among members that relates to their purpose and guides and obligates how they must work together.

No group ever becomes a team until it can hold itself accountable as a team. Like common purpose and approach, mutual accountability is a stiff test. Think, for example, about the subtle but critical difference between "the boss holds me accountable" and "we hold ourselves accountable." The first case can lead to the second, but without the second, there can be no team.

Companies like Hewlett-Packard and Motorola have an ingrained performance ethic that enables teams to form organically whenever there is a clear performance challenge requiring collective rather than individual effort. In these companies, the factor of mutual accountability is commonplace. "Being in the boat together" is how their performance game is played.

At its core, team accountability is about the sincere promises we make to ourselves and others, promises that underpin two critical aspects of effective teams: commitment and trust. Most of us enter a potential team situation cautiously because ingrained individualism and experience discourage us from putting our fates in the hands of others or accepting responsibility for others. Teams do not succeed by ignoring or wishing away such behavior.

Mutual accountability cannot be coerced any more than people can be made to trust one another. But when a team shares a common purpose, goals, and approach, mutual accountability grows as a natural counterpart. Accountability arises from and reinforces the time, energy, and action invested in figuring out what the team is trying to accomplish and how best to get it done.

When people work together toward a common objective, trust and commitment follow. Consequently, teams enjoying a strong common purpose and approach inevitably hold themselves responsible, both as individuals and as a team, for the team's performance. This sense of mutual accountability also produces the rich rewards of mutual achievement in which all members share. What we heard over and over from members of effective teams is that they found the experience energizing and motivating in ways that their "normal" jobs never could match.

On the other hand, groups established primarily for the sake of becoming a team or for job enhancement, communication, organizational effectiveness, or excellence rarely become effective teams, as demonstrated by the bad feelings left in many companies after experimenting with quality circles that never translated "quality" into specific goals. Only when appropriate performance goals are set does the process of discussing the goals and the approaches to them give team members a clearer and clearer choice: They can disagree with a goal and the path that the team selects and, in effect, opt out, or they can pitch in and become accountable with and to their teammates.

The discipline of teams we've outlined is critical to the success of all teams. Yet it is also useful to go one step further. Most teams can be classified in one of three ways: teams that recommend things, teams that make or do things, and teams that run things. In our experience, each type faces a characteristic set of challenges.

Teams That Recommend Things

These teams include task forces; project groups; and audit, quality, or safety groups asked to study and solve particular problems. Teams that recommend things almost always have predetermined completion dates. Two critical issues are unique to such teams:

getting off to a fast and constructive start and dealing with the ulti-mate handoff that's required to get recommendations implemented.

The key to the first issue lies in the clarity of the team's charter and the composition of its membership. In addition to wanting to know why and how their efforts are important, task forces need a clear definition of whom management expects to participate and the time commitment required. Management can help by ensuring that the team includes people with the skills and influence necessary for crafting practical recommendations that will carry weight through-out the organization. Moreover, management can help the team get the necessary cooperation by opening doors and dealing with politi-cal obstacles.

Missing the handoff is almost always the problem that stymies teams that recommend things. To avoid this, the transfer of respon-sibility for recommendations to those who must implement them demands top management's time and attention. The more top man-agers assume that recommendations will "just happen," the less likely it is that they will. The more involvement task force members have in implementing their recommendations, the more likely they are to get implemented.

To the extent that people outside the task force will have to carry the ball, it is critical to involve them in the process early and often, certainly well before recommendations are finalized. Such involve-ment may take many forms, including participating in interviews, helping with analyses, contributing and critiquing ideas, and conducting experiments and trials. At a minimum, anyone responsi-ble for implementation should receive a briefing on the task force's purpose, approach, and objectives at the beginning of the effort as well as regular reviews of progress.

Teams That Make or Do Things

These teams include people at or near the front lines who are responsible for doing the basic manufacturing, development, opera-tions, marketing, sales, service, and other value-adding activities of a business. With some exceptions, such as new-product development or process design teams, teams that make or do things tend to have no set completion dates because their activities are ongoing.

In deciding where team performance might have the greatest impact, top management should concentrate on what we call the company's "critical delivery points"—that is, places in the organization where the cost and value of the company's products and services are most directly determined. Such critical delivery points might include where accounts get managed, customer service performed, products designed, and productivity determined. If performance at critical delivery points depends on combining multiple skills, perspectives, and judgments in real time, then the team option is the smartest one.

When an organization does require a significant number of teams at these points, the sheer challenge of maximizing the performance of so many groups will demand a carefully constructed and performance-focused set of management processes. The issue here for top management is how to build the necessary systems and process supports without falling into the trap of appearing to promote teams for their own sake.

The imperative here, returning to our earlier discussion of the basic discipline of teams, is a relentless focus on performance. If management fails to pay persistent attention to the link between teams and performance, the organization becomes convinced that "this year, we are doing 'teams'." Top management can help by instituting processes like pay schemes and training for teams responsive to their real time needs, but more than anything else, top management must make clear and compelling demands on the teams themselves and then pay constant attention to their progress with respect to both team basics and performance results. This means focusing on specific teams and specific performance challenges. Otherwise "performance," like "team," will become a cliché.

Teams That Run Things

Despite the fact that many leaders refer to the group reporting to them as a team, few groups really are. And groups that become real teams seldom think of themselves as a team because they are so focused on performance results. Yet the opportunity for such teams includes groups from the top of the enterprise down through the divisional or functional level. Whether it is in charge of thousands of people or just a handful, as long as the group oversees some business, ongoing program, or significant functional activity, it is a team that runs things.

The main issue these teams face is determining whether a real team approach is the right one. Many groups that run things can be more effective as working groups than as teams. The key judgment is whether the sum of individual bests will suffice for the performance challenge at hand or whether the group must deliver substantial incremental performance requiring real joint work products. Although the team option promises greater performance, it also brings more risk, and managers must be brutally honest in assessing the trade-offs.

Members may have to overcome a natural reluctance to trust their fate to others. The price of faking the team approach is high: At best, members get diverted from their individual goals, costs outweigh benefits, and people resent the imposition on their time and priorities. At worst, serious animosities develop that undercut even the potential personal bests of the working-group approach.

Working groups present fewer risks. Effective working groups need little time to shape their purpose, since the leader usually establishes it. Meetings are run against well-prioritized agendas. And decisions are implemented through specific individual assignments and accountabilities. Most of the time, therefore, if performance aspirations can be met through individuals doing their respective jobs well, the working-group approach is more comfortable, less risky, and less disruptive than trying for more elusive team performance levels. Indeed, if there is no performance need for the team approach, efforts spent to improve the effectiveness of the working group make much more sense than floundering around trying to become a team.

Having said that, we believe the extra level of performance teams can achieve is becoming critical for a growing number of companies, especially as they move through major changes during which company performance depends on broad-based behavioral change. When top management uses teams to run things, it should make sure the team succeeds in identifying specific purposes and goals.

This is a second major issue for teams that run things. Too often, such teams confuse the broad mission of the total organization with the specific purpose of their small group at the top. The discipline of teams tells us that for a real team to form, there must be a team purpose that is distinctive and specific to the small group and that requires its members to roll up their sleeves and accomplish something beyond individual end products. If a group of managers looks only at the economic performance of the part of the organization it runs to assess overall effectiveness, the group will not have any team performance goals of its own.

While the basic discipline of teams does not differ for them, teams at the top are certainly the most difficult. The complexities of long-term challenges, heavy demands on executive time, and the deep-seated individualism of senior people conspire against teams at the top. At the same time, teams at the top are the most powerful. At first we thought such teams were nearly impossible. That is because we were looking at the teams as defined by the formal organizational structure; that is, the leader and all his or her direct reports equals the team. Then we discovered that real teams at the top were often smaller and less formalized: Whitehead and Weinberg at Goldman Sachs; Hewlett and Packard at HP; Krasnoff, Pall, and Hardy at Pall Corporation; Kendall, Pearson, and Calloway at Pepsi; Haas and Haas at Levi Strauss; Batten and Ridder at Knight Ridder. They were mostly twos and threes, with an occasional fourth.

Nonetheless, real teams at the top of large, complex organizations are still few and far between. Far too many groups at the top of large corporations needlessly constrain themselves from achieving real team levels of performance because they assume that all direct reports must be on the team, that team goals must be identical to corporate goals, that the team members' positions rather than skills determine their respective roles, that a team must be a team all the time, and that the team leader is above doing real work.

As understandable as these assumptions may be, most of them are unwarranted. They do not apply to the teams at the top we have observed, and when replaced with more realistic and flexible assumptions that permit the team discipline to be applied, real team performance at the top can and does occur. Moreover, as more and more companies are confronted with the need to manage major change across their organizations, we will see more real teams at the top.

We believe that teams will become the primary unit of performance in high-performance organizations. But that does not mean that teams will crowd out individual opportunity or formal hierarchy and process. Rather, teams will enhance existing structures without replacing them. A team opportunity exists anywhere hierarchy or organizational boundaries inhibit the skills and perspectives needed for optimal results. Thus, new-product innovation requires preserving functional excellence through structure while eradicating functional bias through teams. And frontline productivity requires preserving direction and guidance through hierarchy while drawing on energy and flexibility through self-managing teams.

We are convinced that every company faces specific performance challenges for which teams are the most practical and powerful vehicle at top management's disposal. The critical role for senior managers, therefore, is to worry about company performance and the kinds of teams that can deliver it. This means top management must recognize a team's unique potential to deliver results, deploy teams strategically when they are the best tool for the job, and foster the basic discipline of teams that will make them effective. By doing so, top management creates the kind of environment that enables team as well as individual and organizational performance.

Originally published in March 1993. Reprint R0507P

Eight Ways to Build Collaborative Teams

by Lynda Gratton and Tamara J. Erickson

WHEN TACKLING A MAJOR initiative like an acquisition or an overhaul of IT systems, companies rely on large, diverse teams of highly educated specialists to get the job done. These teams often are convened quickly to meet an urgent need and work together virtually, collaborating online and sometimes over long distances.

Appointing such a team is frequently the only way to assemble the knowledge and breadth required to pull off many of the complex tasks businesses face today. When the BBC covers the World Cup or the Olympics, for instance, it gathers a large team of researchers, writers, producers, cameramen, and technicians, many of whom have not met before the project. These specialists work together under the high pressure of a "no retake" environment, with just one chance to record the action. Similarly, when the central IT team at Marriott sets out to develop sophisticated systems to enhance guest experiences, it has to collaborate closely with independent hotel owners, customer-experience experts, global brand managers, and regional heads, each with his or her own agenda and needs.

Our recent research into team behavior at 15 multinational companies, however, reveals an interesting paradox: Although teams that are large, virtual, diverse, and composed of highly educated specialists are increasingly crucial with challenging projects, those same four characteristics make it hard for teams to get anything done. To put it another way, the qualities required for success are the same qualities that undermine success. Members of complex teams are less likely—*absent other influences*—to share knowledge freely, to learn from one another, to shift workloads flexibly to break up unexpected bottlenecks, to help one another complete jobs and meet deadlines, and to share resources—in other words, to collaborate. They are less likely to say that they "sink or swim" together, want one another to succeed, or view their goals as compatible.

Consider the issue of size. Teams have grown considerably over the past ten years. New technologies help companies extend participation on a project to an ever greater number of people, allowing firms to tap into a wide body of knowledge and expertise. A decade or so ago, the common view was that true teams rarely had more than 20 members. Today, according to our research, many complex tasks involve teams of 100 or more. However, as the size of a team increases beyond 20 members, the tendency to collaborate naturally decreases, we have found. Under the right conditions, large teams can achieve high levels of cooperation, but creating those conditions requires thoughtful, and sometimes significant, investments in the capacity for collaboration across the organization.

Working together virtually has a similar impact on teams. The majority of those we studied had members spread among multiple locations—in several cases, in as many as 13 sites around the globe. But as teams became more virtual, we saw, cooperation also declined, unless the company had taken measures to establish a collaborative culture.

As for diversity, the challenging tasks facing businesses today almost always require the input and expertise of people with disparate views and backgrounds to create cross-fertilization that sparks insight and innovation. But diversity also creates problems. Our research shows that team members collaborate more easily and naturally if they perceive themselves as being alike. The differences that inhibit collaboration include not only nationality but also age, educational level, and even tenure. Greater diversity also often

Idea in Brief

To execute major initiatives in your organization—integrating a newly acquired firm, overhauling an IT system—you need **complex** teams. Such teams' defining characteristics—large, virtual, diverse, and specialized—are crucial for handling daunting projects. Yet these very characteristics can also destroy team members' ability to work together, say Gratton and Erickson. For instance, as team size grows, collaboration diminishes.

To maximize your complex teams' effectiveness, construct a basis for collaboration in your company.

Eight practices hinging on relationship building and cultural change can help. For example, create a strong sense of community by sponsoring events and activities that bring people together and help them get to know one another. And use informal mentoring and coaching to encourage employees to view interaction with leaders and colleagues as valuable.

When executives, HR professionals, and team leaders all pitch in to apply these practices, complex teams hit the ground running—the day they're formed.

means that team members are working with people that they know only superficially or have never met before—colleagues drawn from other divisions of the company, perhaps, or even from outside it. We have found that the higher the proportion of strangers on the team and the greater the diversity of background and experience, the less likely the team members are to share knowledge or exhibit other collaborative behaviors.

In the same way, the higher the educational level of the team members is, the more challenging collaboration appears to be for them. We found that the greater the proportion of experts a team had, the more likely it was to disintegrate into nonproductive conflict or stalemate.

So how can executives strengthen an organization's ability to perform complex collaborative tasks—to maximize the effectiveness of large, diverse teams, while minimizing the disadvantages posed by their structure and composition?

To answer that question we looked carefully at 55 large teams and identified those that demonstrated high levels of collaborative behavior despite their complexity. Put differently, they succeeded

Idea in Practice

The authors recommend these practices for encouraging collaboration in complex teams.

What Executives Can Do

- Invest in building and maintaining social relationships throughout your organization.

  Example: Royal Bank of Scotland's CEO commissioned new headquarters built around an indoor atrium and featuring a "Main Street" with shops, picnic spaces, and a leisure club. The design encourages employees to rub shoulders daily, which fuels collaboration in RBS's complex teams.

- Model collaborative behavior.

  Example: At Standard Chartered Bank, top executives frequently fill in for one another, whether leading regional celebrations, representing SCB at key external events, or initiating internal dialogues with employees. They make their collaborative behavior visible through extensive travel and photos of leaders from varied sites working together.

- Use coaching to reinforce a collaborative culture.

  Example: At Nokia, each new hire's manager lists everyone in the organization the newcomer should meet, suggests topics he or she should discuss with each person on the list, and explains why establishing each of these relationships is important.

What HR Can Do

- Train employees in the specific skills required for collaboration: appreciating others, engaging in purposeful conversation,

both because of and despite their composition. Using a range of statistical analyses, we considered how more than 100 factors, such as the design of the task and the company culture, might contribute to collaboration, manifested, for example, in a willingness to share knowledge and workloads. Out of the 100-plus factors, we were able to isolate eight practices that correlated with success— that is, that appeared to help teams overcome substantially the difficulties that were posed by size, long-distance communication, diversity, and specialization. We then interviewed the teams that were very strong in these practices, to find out how they did it. In this article we'll walk through the practices. They fall into four productively and creatively resolving conflicts, and managing programs.

- Support a sense of community by sponsoring events and activities such as networking groups, cooking weekends, or tennis coaching. Spontaneous, unannounced activities can further foster community spirit.

Example: Marriott has recognized the anniversary of the company's first hotel opening by rolling back the cafeteria to the 1950s and sponsoring a team twist dance contest.

What Team Leaders Can Do

- Ensure that at least 20%–40% of a new team's members already know one another.

Example: When Nokia needs to transfer skills across business functions or units, it moves entire small teams intact instead of reshuffling individual people into new positions.

- Change your leadership style as your team develops. At early stages in the project, be task-oriented: articulate the team's goal and accountabilities. As inevitable conflicts start emerging, switch to relationship building.

- Assign distinct roles so team members can do their work independently. They'll spend less time negotiating responsibilities or protecting turf. But leave the *path* to achieving the team's goal somewhat ambiguous. Lacking well-defined tasks, members are more likely to invest time and energy collaborating.

general categories—executive support, HR practices, the strength of the team leader, and the structure of the team itself.

Executive Support

At the most basic level, a team's success or failure at collaborating reflects the philosophy of top executives in the organization. Teams do well when executives invest in supporting social relationships, demonstrate collaborative behavior themselves, and create what we call a "gift culture"—one in which employees experience interactions with leaders and colleagues as something valuable and generously offered, a gift.

Investing in signature relationship practices

When we looked at complex collaborative teams that were perform-ing in a productive and innovative manner, we found that in every case the company's top executives had invested significantly in build-ing and maintaining social relationships throughout the organization. However, the way they did that varied widely. The most collaborative companies had what we call "signature" practices—practices that were memorable, difficult for others to replicate, and particularly well suited to their own business environment.

For example, when Royal Bank of Scotland's CEO, Fred Goodwin, invested £350 million to open a new headquarters building outside Edinburgh in 2005, one of his goals was to foster productive collabo-ration among employees. Built around an indoor atrium, the new structure allows more than 3,000 people from the firm to rub shoul-ders daily.

The headquarters is designed to improve communication, increase the exchange of ideas, and create a sense of community among employees. Many of the offices have an open layout and look over the atrium—a vast transparent space. The campus is set up like a small town, with retail shops, restaurants, jogging tracks and cycling trails, spaces for picnics and barbecues—even a leisure club complete with swimming pool, gym, dance studios, tennis courts, and football pitches. The idea is that with a private "Main Street" running through the headquarters, employees will remain on the campus throughout the day—and be out of their offices mingling with colleagues for at least a portion of it.

To ensure that non-headquarters staff members feel they are a part of the action, Goodwin also commissioned an adjoining busi-ness school, where employees from other locations meet and learn. The visitors are encouraged to spend time on the headquarters cam-pus and at forums designed to give employees opportunities to build relationships.

Indeed, the RBS teams we studied had very strong social relation-ships, a solid basis for collaborative activity that allowed them to accomplish tasks quickly. Take the Group Business Improvement (GBI) teams, which work on 30-, 60-, or 90-day projects ranging from back-office fixes to IT updates and are made up of people from across RBS's many businesses, including insurance, retail banking, and private banking in Europe and the United States. When RBS bought NatWest and migrated the new acquisition's technology platform to RBS's, the speed and success of the GBI teams confounded many market analysts.

BP has made another sort of signature investment. Because its employees are located all over the world, with relatively few at headquarters, the company aims to build social networks by moving employees across functions, businesses, and countries as part of their career development. When BP integrates an acquisition (it has grown by buying numerous smaller oil companies), the leadership development committee deliberately rotates employees from the acquired firm through positions across the corporation. Though the easier and cheaper call would be to leave the executives in their own units—where, after all, they know the business—BP instead trains them to take on new roles. As a consequence any senior team today is likely to be made up of people from multiple heritages. Changing roles frequently—it would not be uncommon for a senior leader at BP to have worked in four businesses and three geographic locations over the past decade—forces executives to become very good at meeting new people and building relationships with them.

Modeling collaborative behavior

In companies with many thousands of employees, relatively few have the opportunity to observe the behavior of the senior team on a day-to-day basis. Nonetheless, we found that the perceived behavior of senior executives plays a significant role in determining how cooperative teams are prepared to be.

Executives at Standard Chartered Bank are exceptionally good role models when it comes to cooperation, a strength that many attribute to the firm's global trading heritage. The Chartered Bank received its remit from Queen Victoria in 1853. The bank's traditional business was in cotton from Bombay (now Mumbai), indigo and tea from Calcutta, rice from Burma, sugar from Java, tobacco from Sumatra, hemp from Manila, and silk from Yokohama. The Standard

The Research

OUR WORK IS BASED on a major research initiative conducted jointly by the Concours Institute (a member of BSG Alliance) and the Cooperative Research Project of London Business School, with funding from the Advanced Institute for Management and 15 corporate sponsors. The initiative was created as a way to explore the practicalities of collaborative work in contemporary organizations.

We sent surveys to 2,420 people, including members of 55 teams. A total of 1,543 people replied, a response rate of 64%. Separate surveys were administered to group members, to group leaders, to the executives who evaluated teams, and to HR leaders at the companies involved. The tasks performed by the teams included new-product development, process reengineering, and identifying new solutions to business problems. The companies involved included four telecommunication companies, seven financial services or consulting firms, two media companies, a hospitality firm, and one oil company. The size of the teams ranged from four to 183 people, with an average of 44.

Our objective was to study the levers that executives could pull to improve team performance and innovation in collaborative tasks. We examined scores of possible factors, including the following.

The general culture of the company. We designed a wide range of survey questions to measure the extent to which the firm had a cooperative culture and to uncover employees' attitudes toward knowledge sharing.

Human resources practices and processes. We studied the way staffing took place and the process by which people were promoted. We examined the

Bank was founded in the Cape Province of South Africa in 1863 and was prominent in financing the development of the diamond fields and later gold mines. Standard Chartered was formed in 1969 through a merger of the two banks, and today the firm has 57 operating groups in 57 countries, with no home market.

It's widely accepted at Standard Chartered that members of the general management committee will frequently serve as substitutes for one another. The executives all know and understand the entire business and can fill in for each other easily on almost any task, whether it's leading a regional celebration, representing the company at a key external event, or kicking off an internal dialogue with employees.

extent and type of training, how reward systems were configured, and the extent to which mentoring and coaching took place.

Socialization and network-building practices. We looked at how often people within the team participated in informal socialization, and the type of interaction that was most common. We also asked numerous questions about the extent to which team members were active in informal communities.

The design of the task. We asked team members and team leaders about the task itself. Our interest here was in how they perceived the purpose of the task, how complex it was, the extent to which the task required members of the team to be interdependent, and the extent to which the task required them to engage in boundary-spanning activities with people outside the team.

The leadership of the team. We studied the perceptions team members had of their leaders' style and how the leaders described their own style. In particular, we were interested in the extent to which the leaders practiced relationship-oriented and task-oriented skills and set cooperative or competitive goals.

The behavior of the senior executives. We asked team members and team leaders about their perceptions of the senior executives of their business unit. We focused in particular on whether team members described them as cooperative or competitive.

In total we considered more than 100 factors. Using a range of statistical analyses, we were able to identify eight that correlated with the successful performance of teams handling complex collaborative tasks.

While the behavior of the executive team is crucial to supporting a culture of collaboration, the challenge is to make executives' behavior visible. At Standard Chartered the senior team travels extensively; the norm is to travel even for relatively brief meetings. This investment in face-to-face interaction creates many opportunities for people across the company to see the top executives in action. Internal communication is frequent and open, and, maybe most telling, every site around the world is filled with photos of groups of executives—country and functional leaders—working together.

The senior team's collaborative nature trickles down throughout the organization. Employees quickly learn that the best way to get things done is through informal networks. For example, when a

Collaboration Conundrums

FOUR TRAITS THAT ARE crucial to teams—but also undermine them.

Large Size
Whereas a decade ago, teams rarely had more than 20 members, our findings show that their size has increased significantly, no doubt because of new technologies. Large teams are often formed to ensure the involvement of a wide stakeholder group, the coordination of a diverse set of activities, and the harnessing of multiple skills. As a consequence, many inevitably involve 100 people or more. However, our research shows that as the size of the team increases beyond 20 members, the level of natural cooperation among members of the team decreases.

Virtual Participation
Today most complex collaborative teams have members who are working at a distance from one another. Again, the logic is that the assigned tasks require the insights and knowledge of people from many locations. Team members may be working in offices in the same city or strung across the world. Only

---

major program was recently launched to introduce a new customer-facing technology, the team responsible had an almost uncanny ability to understand who the key stakeholders at each branch bank were and how best to approach them. The team members' first-name acquaintance with people across the company brought a sense of dynamism to their interactions.

Creating a "gift culture"
A third important role for executives is to ensure that mentoring and coaching become embedded in their own routine behavior—and throughout the company. We looked at both formal mentoring processes, with clear roles and responsibilities, and less formal processes, where mentoring was integrated into everyday activities. It turned out that while both types were important, the latter was more likely to increase collaborative behavior. Daily coaching helps establish a cooperative "gift culture" in place of a more transactional "tit-for-tat culture."

At Nokia informal mentoring begins as soon as someone steps into a new job. Typically, within a few days, the employee's manager will

40% of the teams in our sample had members all in one place. Our research shows that as teams become more virtual, collaboration declines.

Diversity

Often the challenging tasks facing today's businesses require the rapid assembly of people from multiple backgrounds and perspectives, many of whom have rarely, if ever, met. Their diverse knowledge and views can spark insight and innovation. However, our research shows that the higher the proportion of people who don't know anyone else on the team and the greater the diversity, the less likely the team members are to share knowledge.

High Education Levels

Complex collaborative teams often generate huge value by drawing on a variety of deeply specialized skills and knowledge to devise new solutions. Again, however, our research shows that the greater the proportion of highly educated specialists on a team, the more likely the team is to disintegrate into unproductive conflicts.

---

sit down and list all the people in the organization, no matter in what location, it would be useful for the employee to meet. This is a deeply ingrained cultural norm, which probably originated when Nokia was a smaller and simpler organization. The manager sits with the newcomer, just as her manager sat with her when she joined, and reviews what topics the newcomer should discuss with each person on the list and why establishing a relationship with him or her is important. It is then standard for the newcomer to actively set up meetings with the people on the list, even when it means traveling to other locations. The gift of time—in the form of hours spent on coaching and building networks—is seen as crucial to the collaborative culture at Nokia.

Focused HR Practices

So what about human resources? Is collaboration solely in the hands of the executive team? In our study we looked at the impact of a wide variety of HR practices, including selection, performance management, promotion, rewards, and training, as well as formally sponsored coaching and mentoring programs.

We found some surprises: for example, that the type of reward system—whether based on team or individual achievement, or tied explicitly to collaborative behavior or not—had no discernible effect on complex teams' productivity and innovation. Although most formal HR programs appeared to have limited impact, we found that two practices did improve team performance: training in skills related to collaborative behavior, and support for informal community building. Where collaboration was strong, the HR team had typically made a significant investment in one or both of those practices—often in ways that uniquely represented the company's culture and business strategy.

Ensuring the requisite skills
Many of the factors that support collaboration relate to what we call the "container" of collaboration—the underlying culture and habits of the company or team. However, we found that some teams had a collaborative culture but were not skilled in the practice of collaboration itself. They were encouraged to cooperate, they wanted to cooperate, but they didn't know how to work together very well in teams.

Our study showed that a number of skills were crucial: appreciating others, being able to engage in purposeful conversations, productively and creatively resolving conflicts, and program management. By training employees in those areas, a company's human resources or corporate learning department can make an important difference in team performance.

In the research, PricewaterhouseCoopers emerged as having one of the strongest capabilities in productive collaboration. With responsibility for developing 140,000 employees in nearly 150 countries, PwC's training includes modules that address teamwork, emotional intelligence, networking, holding difficult conversations, coaching, corporate social responsibility, and communicating the firm's strategy and shared values. PwC also teaches employees how to influence others effectively and build healthy partnerships.

A number of other successful teams in our sample came from organizations that had a commitment to teaching employees

Eight Factors That Lead to Success

1. **Investing in signature relationship practices.** Executives can encourage collaborative behavior by making highly visible investments—in facilities with open floor plans to foster communication, for example—that demonstrate their commitment to collaboration.

2. **Modeling collaborative behavior.** At companies where the senior executives demonstrate highly collaborative behavior themselves, teams collaborate well.

3. **Creating a "gift culture."** Mentoring and coaching—especially on an informal basis—help people build the networks they need to work across corporate boundaries.

4. **Ensuring the requisite skills.** Human resources departments that teach employees how to build relationships, communicate well, and resolve conflicts creatively can have a major impact on team collaboration.

5. **Supporting a strong sense of community.** When people feel a sense of community, they are more comfortable reaching out to others and more likely to share knowledge.

6. **Assigning team leaders that are both task- and relationship-oriented.** The debate has traditionally focused on whether a task or a relationship orientation creates better leadership, but in fact both are key to successfully leading a team. Typically, leaning more heavily on a task orientation at the outset of a project and shifting toward a relationship orientation once the work is in full swing works best.

7. **Building on heritage relationships.** When too many team members are strangers, people may be reluctant to share knowledge. The best practice is to put at least a few people who know one another on the team.

8. **Understanding role clarity and task ambiguity.** Cooperation increases when the roles of individual team members are sharply defined yet the team is given latitude on how to achieve the task.

relationship skills. Lehman Brothers' flagship program for its client-facing staff, for instance, is its training in selling and relationship management. The program is not about sales techniques but, rather, focuses on how Lehman values its clients and makes sure that every client has access to all the resources the firm has to offer.

It is essentially a course on strategies for building collaborative partnerships with customers, emphasizing the importance of trust-based personal relationships.

Supporting a sense of community

While a communal spirit can develop spontaneously, we discovered that HR can also play a critical role in cultivating it, by sponsoring group events and activities such as women's networks, cooking weekends, and tennis coaching, or creating policies and practices that encourage them.

At ABN Amro we studied effective change-management teams within the company's enterprise services function. These informal groups were responsible for projects associated with the implementation of new technology throughout the bank; one team, for instance, was charged with expanding online banking services. To succeed, the teams needed the involvement and expertise of different parts of the organization.

The ABN Amro teams rated the company's support for informal communities very positively. The firm makes the technology needed for long-distance collaboration readily available to groups of individuals with shared interests—for instance, in specific technologies or markets—who hold frequent web conferences and communicate actively online. The company also encourages employees that travel to a new location to arrange meetings with as many people as possible. As projects are completed, working groups disband but employees maintain networks of connections. These practices serve to build a strong community over time—one that sets the stage for success with future projects.

Committed investment in informal networks is also a central plank of the HR strategy at Marriott. Despite its size and global reach, Marriott remains a family business, and the chairman, Bill Marriott, makes a point of communicating that idea regularly to employees. He still tells stories of counting sticky nickels at night as a child—proceeds from the root-beer stand founded in downtown Washington, DC, by his mother and father.

How Complex Is the Collaborative Task?

NOT ALL HIGHLY COLLABORATIVE tasks are complex. In assembling and managing a team, consider the project you need to assign and whether the following statements apply:

- The task is unlikely to be accomplished successfully using only the skills within the team.

- The task must be addressed by a new group formed specifically for this purpose.

- The task requires collective input from highly specialized individuals.

- The task requires collective input and agreement from more than 20 people.

- The members of the team working on the task are in more than two locations.

- The success of the task is highly dependent on understanding preferences or needs of individuals outside the group.

- The outcome of the task will be influenced by events that are highly uncertain and difficult to predict.

- The task must be completed under extreme time pressure.

If more than two of these statements are true, the task requires complex collaboration.

Many of the firm's HR investments reinforce a friendly, family-like culture. Almost every communication reflects an element of staff appreciation. A range of "pop-up" events—spontaneous activities—create a sense of fun and community. For example, the cafeteria might roll back to the 1950s, hold a twist dance contest, and in doing so, recognize the anniversary of the company's first hotel opening. Bill Marriott's birthday might be celebrated with parties throughout the company, serving as an occasion to emphasize the firm's culture and values. The chairman recently began his own blog, which is popular with employees, in which he discusses everything from Marriott's efforts to become greener, to his favorite family vacation spots—themes intended to reinforce the idea that the company is a community.

The Right Team Leaders

In the groups that had high levels of collaborative behavior, the team leaders clearly made a significant difference. The question in our minds was how they actually achieved this. The answer, we saw, lay in their flexibility as managers.

Assigning leaders who are both task- and relationship-oriented

There has been much debate among both academics and senior managers about the most appropriate style for leading teams. Some people have suggested that relationship-oriented leadership is most appropriate in complex teams, since people are more likely to share knowledge in an environment of trust and goodwill. Others have argued that a task orientation—the ability to make objectives clear, to create a shared awareness of the dimensions of the task, and to provide monitoring and feedback—is most important.

In the 55 teams we studied, we found that the truth lay somewhere in between. The most productive, innovative teams were typically led by people who were *both* task- and relationship-oriented. What's more, these leaders changed their style during the project. Specifically, at the early stages they exhibited task-oriented leadership: They made the goal clear, engaged in debates about commitments, and clarified the responsibilities of individual team members. However, at a certain point in the development of the project they switched to a relationship orientation. This shift often took place once team members had nailed down the goals and their accountabilities and when the initial tensions around sharing knowledge had begun to emerge. An emphasis throughout a project on one style at the expense of the other inevitably hindered the long-term performance of the team, we found.

Producing ambidextrous team leaders—those with both relationship and task skills—is a core goal of team-leadership development at Marriott. The company's performance-review process emphasizes growth in both kinds of skills. As evidence of their relationship skills, managers are asked to describe their peer network and cite examples of specific ways that network helped them succeed. They also must provide examples of how they've used relationship building to get things done. The development plans that follow these conversations explicitly map out how the managers can improve specific elements of their social relationships and networks. Such a plan might include, for instance, having lunch regularly with people from a particular community of interest.

To improve their task leadership, many people in the teams at Marriott participated in project-management certification programs, taking refresher courses to maintain their skills over time. Evidence of both kinds of capabilities becomes a significant criterion on which people are selected for key leadership roles at the company.

Team Formation and Structure

The final set of lessons for developing and managing complex teams has to do with the makeup and structure of the teams themselves.

Building on heritage relationships

Given how important trust is to successful collaboration, forming teams that capitalize on preexisting, or "heritage," relationships, increases the chances of a project's success. Our research shows that new teams, particularly those with a high proportion of members who were strangers at the time of formation, find it more difficult to collaborate than those with established relationships.

Newly formed teams are forced to invest significant time and effort in building trusting relationships. However, when some team members already know and trust one another, they can become nodes, which over time evolve into networks. Looking closely at our data, we discovered that when 20% to 40% of the team members were already well connected to one another, the team had strong collaboration right from the start.

It helps, of course, if the company leadership has taken other measures to cultivate networks that cross boundaries. The orientation process at Nokia ensures that a large number of people on any team know one another, increasing the odds that even in a company of more than 100,000 people, someone on a companywide team knows someone else and can make introductions.

Nokia has also developed an organizational architecture designed to make good use of heritage relationships. When it needs to transfer skills across business functions or units, Nokia moves entire small teams intact instead of reshuffling individual people into new positions. If, for example, the company needs to bring together a group of market and technology experts to address a new customer need, the group formed would be composed of small pods of colleagues from each area. This ensures that key heritage relationships continue to strengthen over time, even as the organization redirects its resources to meet market needs. Because the entire company has one common platform for logistics, HR, finance, and other transactions, teams can switch in and out of businesses and geographies without learning new systems.

One important caveat about heritage relationships: If not skillfully managed, too many of them can actually disrupt collaboration. When a significant number of people within the team know one another, they tend to form strong subgroups—whether by function, geography, or anything else they have in common. When that happens, the probability of conflict among the subgroups, which we call fault lines, increases.

Understanding role clarity and task ambiguity

Which is more important to promoting collaboration: a clearly defined approach toward achieving the goal, or clearly specified roles for individual team members? The common assumption is that carefully spelling out the approach is essential, but leaving the roles of individuals within the team vague will encourage people to share ideas and contribute in multiple dimensions.

Our research shows that the opposite is true: Collaboration improves when the roles of individual team members are clearly defined and well understood—when individuals feel that they can do a significant portion of their work independently. Without such clarity, team members are likely to waste too much energy negotiating roles or protecting turf, rather than focus on the task. In addition, team members are more likely to want to collaborate if the path to achieving the team's goal is left somewhat ambiguous. If a team perceives the task as one that requires creativity, where the approach is not yet well known or predefined, its members are more likely to invest time and energy in collaboration.

At the BBC we studied the teams responsible for the radio and television broadcasts of the 2006 Proms (a two-month-long musical celebration), the team that televised the 2006 World Cup, and a team responsible for daytime television news. These teams were large—133 people worked on the Proms, 66 on the World Cup, and 72 on the news—and included members with a wide range of skills and from many disciplines. One would imagine, therefore, that there was a strong possibility of confusion among team members.

To the contrary, we found that the BBC's teams scored among the highest in our sample with regard to the clarity with which members viewed their own roles and the roles of others. Every team was composed of specialists who had deep expertise in their given function, and each person had a clearly defined role. There was little overlap between the responsibilities of the sound technician and the camera operator, and so on. Yet the tasks the BBC teams tackle are, by their very nature, uncertain, particularly when they involve breaking news. The trick the BBC has pulled off has been to clarify team members' individual roles with so much precision that it keeps friction to a minimum.

The successful teams we studied at Reuters worked out of far-flung locations, and often the team members didn't speak a common language. (The primary languages were Russian, Chinese, Thai, and English.) These teams, largely composed of software programmers, were responsible for the rapid development of highly complex technical software and network products. Many of the programmers sat at their desks for 12 hours straight developing code, speaking with no one. Ironically, these teams judged cooperative behavior to be high among their members. That may be because each individual was given autonomy over one discrete piece of the project. The rapid pace and demanding project timelines encouraged individual members to work independently to get the job done, but each person's work had to be shaped with an eye toward the overall team goal.

Strengthening your organization's capacity for collaboration requires a combination of long-term investments—in building relationships and trust, in developing a culture in which senior leaders are role models of cooperation—and smart near-term decisions about the ways teams are formed, roles are defined, and challenges and tasks are articulated. Practices and structures that may have worked well with simple teams of people who were all in one location and knew one another are likely to lead to failure when teams grow more complex.

Most of the factors that impede collaboration today would have impeded collaboration at any time in history. Yesterday's teams, however, didn't require the same amount of members, diversity, long-distance cooperation, or expertise that teams now need to solve global business challenges. So the models for teams need to be realigned with the demands of the current business environment. Through careful attention to the factors we've described in this article, companies can assemble the breadth of expertise needed to solve complex business problems—without inducing the destructive behaviors that can accompany it.

Originally published in November 2007. Reprint R0711F

The Power
of Small Wins

Want to truly engage your workers? Help them see their own progress. *by Teresa M. Amabile and Steven J. Kramer*

WHAT IS THE BEST WAY to drive innovative work inside organizations? Important clues hide in the stories of world-renowned creators. It turns out that ordinary scientists, marketers, programmers, and other unsung knowledge workers, whose jobs require creative productivity every day, have more in common with famous innovators than most managers realize. The workday events that ignite their emotions, fuel their motivation, and trigger their perceptions are fundamentally the same.

The Double Helix, James Watson's 1968 memoir about discovering the structure of DNA, describes the roller coaster of emotions he and Francis Crick experienced through the progress and setbacks of the work that eventually earned them the Nobel Prize. After the excitement of their first attempt to build a DNA model, Watson and Crick noticed some serious flaws. According to Watson, "Our first minutes with the models...were not joyous." Later that evening, "a shape began to emerge which brought back our spirits." But when they showed their "breakthrough" to colleagues, they found that their model would not work. Dark days of doubt and ebbing motivation followed. When the duo finally had their bona fide breakthrough, and their colleagues found no fault with it, Watson wrote, "My morale skyrocketed, for I suspected that we now had the answer to the riddle." Watson and Crick were so driven by this success that they practically lived in the lab, trying to complete the work.

Throughout these episodes, Watson and Crick's progress—or lack thereof—ruled their reactions. In our recent research on creative work inside businesses, we stumbled upon a remarkably similar phenomenon. Through exhaustive analysis of diaries kept by knowledge workers, we discovered the *progress principle:* Of all the things that can boost emotions, motivation, and perceptions during a workday, the single most important is making progress in meaningful work. And the more frequently people experience that sense of progress, the more likely they are to be creatively productive in the long run. Whether they are trying to solve a major scientific mystery or simply produce a high-quality product or service, everyday progress—even a small win—can make all the difference in how they feel and perform.

The power of progress is fundamental to human nature, but few managers understand it or know how to leverage progress to boost motivation. In fact, work motivation has been a subject of long-standing debate. In a survey asking about the keys to motivating workers, we found that some managers ranked recognition for good work as most important, while others put more stock in tangible incentives. Some focused on the value of interpersonal support, while still others thought clear goals were the answer. Interestingly, very few of our surveyed managers ranked progress first. (See the sidebar "A Surprise for Managers.")

If you are a manager, the progress principle holds clear implications for where to focus your efforts. It suggests that you have more influence than you may realize over employees' well-being, motivation, and creative output. Knowing what serves to catalyze and nourish progress—and what does the opposite—turns out to be the key to effectively managing people and their work.

In this article, we share what we have learned about the power of progress and how managers can leverage it. We spell out how a focus on progress translates into concrete managerial actions and provide

Idea in Brief

What is the best way to motivate employees to do creative work? Help them take a step forward every day. In an analysis of knowledge workers' diaries, the authors found that nothing contributed more to a positive inner work life (the mix of emotions, motivations, and perceptions that is critical to performance) than making progress in meaningful work. If a person is motivated and happy at the end of the workday, it's a good bet that he or she achieved something, however small. If the person drags out of the office disengaged and joyless, a setback is likely to blame. This progress principle suggests that managers have more influence than they may realize over employees' well-being, motivation, and creative output.

The key is to learn which actions support progress—such as setting clear goals, providing sufficient time and resources, and offering recognition—and which have the opposite effect. Even small wins can boost inner work life tremendously. On the flip side, small losses or setbacks can have an extremely negative effect. And the work doesn't need to involve curing cancer in order to be meaningful. It simply must matter to the person doing it. The actions that set in motion the positive feedback loop between progress and inner work life may sound like Management 101, but it takes discipline to establish new habits. The authors provide a checklist that managers can use on a daily basis to monitor their progress-enhancing behaviors.

Have fun + celebrate wins

a checklist to help make such behaviors habitual. But to clarify why those actions are so potent, we first describe our research and what the knowledge workers' diaries revealed about their *inner work lives*.

Inner Work Life and Performance

For nearly 15 years, we have been studying the psychological experiences and the performance of people doing complex work inside organizations. Early on, we realized that a central driver of creative, productive performance was the quality of a person's inner work life—the mix of emotions, motivations, and perceptions over the course of a workday. How happy workers feel; how motivated they are by an intrinsic interest in the work; how positively they view their organization, their management, their team, their work, and

A Surprise for Managers

IN A 1968 ISSUE OF HBR, Frederick Herzberg published a now-classic article titled "One More Time: How Do You Motivate Employees?" Our findings are consistent with his message: People are most satisfied with their jobs (and therefore most motivated) when those jobs give them the opportunity to experience achievement.

The diary research we describe in this article—in which we microscopically examined the events of thousands of workdays, in real time—uncovered the mechanism underlying the sense of achievement: making consistent, meaningful progress.

But managers seem not to have taken Herzberg's lesson to heart. To assess contemporary awareness of the importance of daily work progress, we recently administered a survey to 669 managers of varying levels from dozens of companies around the world. We asked about the managerial tools that can affect employees' motivation and emotions. The respondents ranked five tools—support for making progress in the work, recognition for good work, incentives, interpersonal support, and clear goals—in order of importance.

Fully 95% of the managers who took our survey would probably be surprised to learn that supporting progress is the primary way to elevate motivation—because that's the percentage that failed to rank progress number one. In fact, only 35 managers ranked progress as the number one motivator—a mere 5%. The vast majority of respondents ranked support for making progress dead last as a motivator and third as an influence on emotion. They ranked "recognition for good work (either public or private)" as the most important factor in motivating workers and making them happy. In our diary study, recognition certainly did boost inner work life. But it wasn't nearly as prominent as progress. Besides, without work achievements, there is little to recognize.

themselves—all these combine either to push them to higher levels of achievement or to drag them down.

To understand such interior dynamics better, we asked members of project teams to respond individually to an end-of-day e-mail survey during the course of the project—just over four months, on average. (For more on this research, see our article "Inner Work Life: Understanding the Subtext of Business Performance," HBR May 2007.) The projects—inventing kitchen gadgets, managing product lines of cleaning tools, and solving complex IT problems for a hotel empire, for example—all involved creativity. The daily survey inquired about participants' emotions and moods, motivation levels, and perceptions of the work environment that day, as well as what work they did and what events stood out in their minds.

Twenty-six project teams from seven companies participated, comprising 238 individuals. This yielded nearly 12,000 diary entries. Naturally, every individual in our population experienced ups and downs. Our goal was to discover the states of inner work life and the workday events that correlated with the highest levels of creative output.

In a dramatic rebuttal to the commonplace claim that high pressure and fear spur achievement, we found that, at least in the realm of knowledge work, people are more creative and productive when their inner work lives are positive—when they feel happy, are intrinsically motivated by the work itself, and have positive perceptions of their colleagues and the organization. Moreover, in those positive states, people are more committed to the work and more collegial toward those around them. Inner work life, we saw, can fluctuate from one day to the next—sometimes wildly—and performance along with it. A person's inner work life on a given day fuels his or her performance for the day and can even affect performance the *next* day.

Once this *inner work life effect* became clear, our inquiry turned to whether and how managerial action could set it in motion. What events could evoke positive or negative emotions, motivations, and perceptions? The answers were tucked within our research participants' diary entries. There are predictable triggers that inflate or deflate inner work life, and, even accounting for variation among individuals, they are pretty much the same for everyone.

The Power of Progress

Our hunt for inner work life triggers led us to the progress principle. When we compared our research participants' best and worst days (based on their overall mood, specific emotions, and motivation levels), we found that the most common event triggering a "best day" was any progress in the work by the individual or the team. The most common event triggering a "worst day" was a setback.

Consider, for example, how progress relates to one component of inner work life: overall mood ratings. Steps forward occurred on 76% of people's best-mood days. By contrast, setbacks occurred on only 13% of those days. (See the exhibit "What happens on a good day?")

Two other types of inner work life triggers also occur frequently on best days: *Catalysts,* actions that directly support work, including help from a person or group, and *nourishers,* events such as shows of respect and words of encouragement. Each has an opposite: *Inhibitors,* actions that fail to support or actively hinder work, and *toxins,* discouraging or undermining events. Whereas catalysts and inhibitors are directed at the project, nourishers and toxins are directed at the person. Like setbacks, inhibitors and toxins are rare on days of great inner work life.

Events on worst-mood days are nearly the mirror image of those on best-mood days (see the exhibit "What happens on a bad day?"). Here, setbacks predominated, occurring on 67% of those days; progress

What happens on a good day?

Progress—even a small step forward—occurs on many of the days people report being in a good mood.

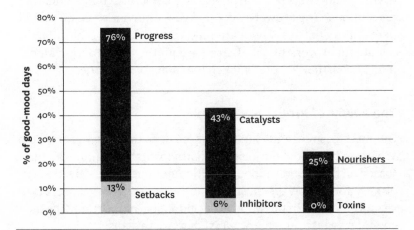

What happens on a bad day?

Events on bad days—setbacks and other hindrances—are nearly the mirror image of those on good days.

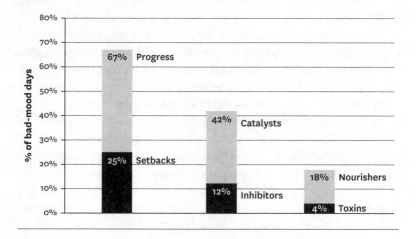

occurred on only 25% of them. Inhibitors and toxins also marked many worst-mood days, and catalysts and nourishers were rare.

This is the progress principle made visible: If a person is motivated and happy at the end of the workday, it's a good bet that he or she made some progress. If the person drags out of the office disengaged and joyless, a setback is most likely to blame.

When we analyzed all 12,000 daily surveys filled out by our participants, we discovered that progress and setbacks influence all three aspects of inner work life. On days when they made progress, our participants reported more positive *emotions*. They not only were in a more upbeat mood in general but also expressed more joy, warmth, and pride. When they suffered setbacks, they experienced more frustration, fear, and sadness.

Motivations were also affected: On progress days, people were more intrinsically motivated—by interest in and enjoyment of the work itself. On setback days, they were not only less intrinsically motivated but also less extrinsically motivated by recognition.

Apparently, setbacks can lead a person to feel generally apathetic and disinclined to do the work at all.

Perceptions differed in many ways, too. On progress days, people perceived significantly more positive challenge in their work. They saw their teams as more mutually supportive and reported more positive interactions between the teams and their supervisors. On a number of dimensions, perceptions suffered when people encountered setbacks. They found less positive challenge in the work, felt that they had less freedom in carrying it out, and reported that they had insufficient resources. On setback days, participants perceived both their teams and their supervisors as less supportive.

To be sure, our analyses establish correlations but do not prove causality. Were these changes in inner work life the result of progress and setbacks, or was the effect the other way around? The numbers alone cannot answer that. However, we do know, from reading thousands of diary entries, that more-positive perceptions, a sense of accomplishment, satisfaction, happiness, and even elation often followed progress. Here's a typical post-progress entry, from a programmer: "I smashed that bug that's been frustrating me for almost a calendar week. That may not be an event to you, but I live a very drab life, so I'm all hyped."

Likewise, we saw that deteriorating perceptions, frustration, sadness, and even disgust often followed setbacks. As another participant, a product marketer, wrote, "We spent a lot of time updating the Cost Reduction project list, and after tallying all the numbers, we are still coming up short of our goal. It is discouraging to not be able to hit it after all the time spent and hard work."

Almost certainly, the causality goes both ways, and managers can use this feedback loop between progress and inner work life to support both.

Minor Milestones

When we think about progress, we often imagine how good it feels to achieve a long-term goal or experience a major breakthrough. These big wins are great—but they are relatively rare. The good news is that even small wins can boost inner work life tremendously. Many of the progress events our research participants reported represented only minor steps forward. Yet they often evoked outsize positive reactions. Consider this diary entry from a programmer in a high-tech company, which was accompanied by very positive self-ratings of her emotions, motivations, and perceptions that day: "I figured out why something was not working correctly. I felt relieved and happy because this was a minor milestone for me."

Even ordinary, incremental progress can increase people's engagement in the work and their happiness during the workday. Across all types of events our participants reported, a notable proportion (28%) of incidents that had a minor impact on the project had a major impact on people's feelings about it. Because inner work life has such a potent effect on creativity and productivity, and because small but consistent steps forward, shared by many people, can accumulate into excellent execution, progress events that often go unnoticed are critical to the overall performance of organizations.

Unfortunately, there is a flip side. Small losses or setbacks can have an extremely negative effect on inner work life. In fact, our study and research by others show that negative events can have a more powerful impact than positive ones. Consequently, it is especially important for managers to minimize daily hassles.

Progress in Meaningful Work

We've shown how gratifying it is for workers when they are able to chip away at a goal, but recall what we said earlier: The key to motivating performance is supporting progress in *meaningful* work. Making headway boosts your inner work life, but only if the work matters to you.

Think of the most boring job you've ever had. Many people nominate their first job as a teenager—washing pots and pans in a restaurant kitchen, for example, or checking coats at a museum. In jobs like those, the power of progress seems elusive. No matter how hard you work, there are always more pots to wash and coats to check; only punching the time clock at the end of the day or getting the paycheck at the end of the week yields a sense of accomplishment.

In jobs with much more challenge and room for creativity, like the ones our research participants had, simply "making progress"— getting tasks done—doesn't guarantee a good inner work life, either. You may have experienced this rude fact in your own job, on days (or in projects) when you felt demotivated, devalued, and frustrated, even though you worked hard and got things done. The likely cause is your perception of the completed tasks as peripheral or irrelevant. For the progress principle to operate, the work must be meaningful to the person doing it.

In 1983, Steve Jobs was trying to entice John Sculley to leave a wildly successful career at PepsiCo to become Apple's new CEO. Jobs reportedly asked him, "Do you want to spend the rest of your life selling sugared water or do you want a chance to change the world?" In making his pitch, Jobs leveraged a potent psychological force: the deep-seated human desire to do meaningful work.

Fortunately, to feel meaningful, work doesn't have to involve putting the first personal computers in the hands of ordinary people, or alleviating poverty, or helping to cure cancer. Work with less profound importance to society can matter if it contributes value to something or someone important to the worker. Meaning can be as simple as making a useful and high-quality product for a customer or providing a genuine service for a community. It can be supporting a colleague or boosting an organization's profits by reducing inefficiencies in a production process. Whether the goals are lofty or modest, as long as they are meaningful to the worker and it is clear how his or her efforts contribute to them, progress toward them can galvanize inner work life.

In principle, managers shouldn't have to go to extraordinary lengths to infuse jobs with meaning. Most jobs in modern organizations are potentially meaningful for the people doing them. However, managers can make sure that employees know just how their work is contributing. And, most important, they can avoid actions that negate its value. (See the sidebar "How Work Gets Stripped of

Its Meaning.") All the participants in our research were doing work that should have been meaningful; no one was washing pots or checking coats. Shockingly often, however, we saw potentially important, challenging work losing its power to inspire.

Supporting Progress: Catalysts and Nourishers

What can managers do to ensure that people are motivated, committed, and happy? How can they support workers' daily progress? They can use catalysts and nourishers, the other kinds of frequent "best day" events we discovered.

Catalysts are actions that support work. They include setting clear goals, allowing autonomy, providing sufficient resources and time, helping with the work, openly learning from problems and successes, and allowing a free exchange of ideas. Their opposites, inhibitors, include failing to provide support and actively interfering with the work. Because of their impact on progress, catalysts and inhibitors ultimately affect inner work life. But they also have a more immediate impact: When people realize that they have clear and meaningful goals, sufficient resources, helpful colleagues, and so on, they get an instant boost to their emotions, their motivation to do a great job, and their perceptions of the work and the organization.

Nourishers are acts of interpersonal support, such as respect and recognition, encouragement, emotional comfort, and opportunities for affiliation. Toxins, their opposites, include disrespect, discouragement, disregard for emotions, and interpersonal conflict. For good and for ill, nourishers and toxins affect inner work life directly and immediately.

Catalysts and nourishers—and their opposites—can alter the meaningfulness of work by shifting people's perceptions of their jobs and even themselves. For instance, when a manager makes sure that people have the resources they need, it signals to them that what they are doing is important and valuable. When managers recognize people for the work they do, it signals that they are important to the organization. In this way, catalysts and nourishers can lend

How Work Gets Stripped of Its Meaning

Diary entries from 238 knowledge workers who were members of creative project teams revealed four primary ways in which managers unwittingly drain work of its meaning.

1. Managers may dismiss the importance of employees' work or ideas. Consider the case of Richard, a senior lab technician at a chemical company, who found meaning in helping his new-product development team solve complex technical problems. However, in team meetings over the course of a three-week period, Richard perceived that his team leader was ignoring his suggestions and those of his teammates. As a result, he felt that his contributions were not meaningful, and his spirits flagged. When at last he believed that he was again making a substantive contribution to the success of the project, his mood improved dramatically:

   > I felt much better at today's team meeting. I felt that my opinions and information were important to the project and that we have made some progress.

2. They may destroy employees' sense of ownership of their work. Frequent and abrupt reassignments often have this effect. This happened repeatedly to the members of a product development team in a giant consumer products company, as described by team member Bruce:

   > As I've been handing over some projects, I do realize that I don't like to give them up. Especially when you have been with them

---

greater meaning to the work—and amplify the operation of the progress principle.

The managerial actions that constitute catalysts and nourishers are not particularly mysterious; they may sound like Management 101, if not just common sense and common decency. But our diary study reminded us how often they are ignored or forgotten. Even some of the more attentive managers in the companies we studied did not consistently provide catalysts and nourishers. For example, a supply-chain specialist named Michael was, in many ways and on most days, an excellent subteam manager. But he was occasionally so overwhelmed that he became toxic toward his people. When a supplier failed to complete a "hot" order on time and Michael's team had to resort to air shipping to meet the customer's deadline, he realized that the profit margin on the sale would be blown. In irritation, he from the start and are nearly to the end. You lose ownership. This happens to us way too often.

3. Managers may send the message that the work employees are doing will never see the light of day. They can signal this—unintentionally—by shifting their priorities or changing their minds about how something should be done. We saw the latter in an internet technology company after user-interface developer Burt had spent weeks designing seamless transitions for non-English-speaking users. Not surprisingly, Burt's mood was seriously marred on the day he reported this incident:

> Other options for the international [interfaces] were [given] to the team during a team meeting, which could render the work I am doing useless.

4. They may neglect to inform employees about unexpected changes in a customer's priorities. Often, this arises from poor customer management or inadequate communication within the company. For example, Stuart, a data transformation expert at an IT company, reported deep frustration and low motivation on the day he learned that weeks of the team's hard work might have been for naught:

> Found out that there is a strong possibility that the project may not be going forward, due to a shift in the client's agenda. Therefore, there is a strong possibility that all the time and effort put into the project was a waste of our time.

lashed out at his subordinates, demeaning the solid work they had done and disregarding their own frustration with the supplier. In his diary, he admitted as much:

> As of Friday, we have spent $28,000 in air freight to send 1,500 $30 spray jet mops to our number two customer. Another 2,800 remain on this order, and there is a good probability that they too will gain wings. I have turned from the kindly Supply Chain Manager into the black-masked executioner. All similarity to civility is gone, our backs are against the wall, flight is not possible, therefore fight is probable.

Even when managers don't have their backs against the wall, developing long-term strategy and launching new initiatives can often seem more important—and perhaps sexier—than making sure that subordinates have what they need to make steady progress and feel supported as human beings. But as we saw repeatedly in our research, even the best strategy will fail if managers ignore the people working in the trenches to execute it.

A Model Manager—And a Tool for Emulating Him

We could explain the many (and largely unsurprising) moves that can catalyze progress and nourish spirits, but it may be more useful to give an example of a manager who consistently used those moves—and then to provide a simple tool that can help any manager do so.

Our model manager is Graham, whom we observed leading a small team of chemical engineers within a multinational European firm we'll call Kruger-Bern. The mission of the team's NewPoly project was clear and meaningful enough: develop a safe, biodegradable polymer to replace petrochemicals in cosmetics and, eventually, in a wide range of consumer products. As in many large firms, however, the project was nested in a confusing and sometimes threatening corporate setting of shifting top-management priorities, conflicting signals, and wavering commitments. Resources were uncomfortably tight, and uncertainty loomed over the project's future—and every team member's career. Even worse, an incident early in the project, in which an important customer reacted angrily to a sample, left the team reeling. Yet Graham was able to sustain team members' inner work lives by repeatedly and visibly removing obstacles, materially supporting progress, and emotionally supporting the team.

Graham's management approach excelled in four ways. First, he established a positive climate, one event at a time, which set behavioral norms for the entire team. When the customer complaint stopped the project in its tracks, for example, he engaged immediately with the team to analyze the problem, without recriminations, and develop a plan for repairing the relationship. In doing so, he modeled how to respond to crises in the work: not by panicking or pointing fingers but by identifying problems and their causes, and developing a coordinated action plan. This is both a practical approach and a great way to give subordinates a sense of forward movement even in the face of the missteps and failures inherent in any complex project.

Second, Graham stayed attuned to his team's everyday activities and progress. In fact, the nonjudgmental climate he had established made this happen naturally. Team members updated him frequently—without being asked—on their setbacks, progress, and plans. At one point, one of his hardest-working colleagues, Brady, had to abort a trial of a new material because he couldn't get the parameters right on the equipment. It was bad news, because the NewPoly team had access to the equipment only one day a week, but Brady immediately informed Graham. In his diary entry that evening, Brady noted, "He didn't like the lost week but seemed to understand." That understanding assured Graham's place in the stream of information that would allow him to give his people just what they needed to make progress.

Third, Graham targeted his support according to recent events in the team and the project. Each day, he could anticipate what type of intervention—a catalyst or the removal of an inhibitor; a nourisher or some antidote to a toxin—would have the most impact on team members' inner work lives and progress. And if he could not make that judgment, he asked. Most days it was not hard to figure out, as on the day he received some uplifting news about his bosses' commitment to the project. He knew the team was jittery about a rumored corporate reorganization and could use the encouragement. Even though the clarification came during a well-earned vacation day, he immediately got on the phone to relay the good news to the team.

Finally, Graham established himself as a resource for team members, rather than a micromanager; he was sure to *check in* while never seeming to *check up* on them. Superficially, checking in and checking up seem quite similar, but micromanagers make four kinds of mistakes. First, they fail to allow autonomy in carrying out the work. Unlike Graham, who gave the NewPoly team a clear strategic goal but respected members' ideas about how to meet it, micromanagers dictate every move. Second, they frequently ask subordinates

The Daily Progress Checklist

Near the end of each workday, use this checklist to review the day and plan your managerial actions for the next day. After a few days, you will be able to identify issues by scanning the boldface words. First, focus on progress and setbacks and think about specific events (catalysts, nourishers, inhibitors, and toxins) that contributed to them. Next, consider any clear inner-work-life clues and what further information they provide about progress and other events. The action plan for the next day is the most important part of your daily review: What is the one thing you can do to best facilitate progress?

Progress

Which 1 or 2 events today indicated either a small win or a possible breakthrough? (Describe briefly.)

_____

_____

Catalysts

☐ Did the team have clear short- and long-term **goals** for meaningful work?

☐ Did team members have sufficient **autonomy** to solve problems and take ownership of the project?

☐ Did they have all the **resources** they needed to move forward efficiently?

☐ Did they have sufficient **time** to focus on meaningful work?

☐ Did I give or get them **help** when they needed or requested it? Did I encourage team members to help one another?

☐ Did I discuss **lessons** from today's successes and problems with my team?

☐ Did I help **ideas** flow freely within the group?

Setbacks

Which 1 or 2 events today indicated either a small setback or a possible crisis? (Describe briefly.)

_____

_____

Inhibitors

☐ Was there any confusion regarding long- or short-term **goals** for meaningful work?

☐ Were team members overly **constrained** in their ability to solve problems and feel ownership of the project?

☐ Did they lack any of the **resources** they needed to move forward effectively?

☐ Did they lack sufficient **time** to focus on meaningful work?

☐ Did I or others fail to provide needed or requested **help**?

☐ Did I "punish" failure or neglect to find **lessons** and/or opportunities in problems and successes?

☐ Did I or others cut off the presentation or debate of **ideas** prematurely?

Nourishers

- [ ] Did I show **respect** to team members by recognizing their contributions to progress, attending to their ideas, and treating them as trusted professionals?

- [ ] Did I **encourage** team members who faced difficult challenges?

- [ ] Did I **support** team members who had a personal or professional problem?

- [ ] Is there a sense of personal and professional **affiliation** and camaraderie within the team?

Toxins

- [ ] Did I **disrespect** any team members by failing to recognize their contributions to progress, not attending to their ideas, or not treating them as trusted professionals?

- [ ] Did I **discourage** a member of the team in any way?

- [ ] Did I **neglect** a team member who had a personal or professional problem?

- [ ] Is there tension or **antagonism** among members of the team or between team members and me?

Inner Work Life

Did I see any indications of the quality of my subordinates' inner work lives today? _____

Perceptions of the work, team, management, firm _____

Emotions _____

Motivation _____

What specific events might have affected inner work life today? _____

Action Plan

What can I do tomorrow to start eliminating the inhibitors and toxins identified?

_____

_____

_____

What can I do tomorrow to strengthen the catalysts and nourishers identified and provide the ones that are lacking?

_____

_____

_____

about their work without providing any real help. By contrast, when one of Graham's team members reported problems, Graham helped analyze them—remaining open to alternative interpretations—and often ended up helping to get things back on track. Third, micromanagers are quick to affix personal blame when problems arise, leading subordinates to hide problems rather than honestly discuss how to surmount them, as Graham did with Brady. And fourth, micromanagers tend to hoard information to use as a secret weapon. Few realize how damaging this is to inner work life. When subordinates perceive that a manager is withholding potentially useful information, they feel infantilized, their motivation wanes, and their work is handicapped. Graham was quick to communicate upper management's views of the project, customers' opinions and needs, and possible sources of assistance or resistance within and outside the organization.

In all those ways, Graham sustained his team's positive emotions, intrinsic motivation, and favorable perceptions. His actions serve as a powerful example of how managers at any level can approach each day determined to foster progress.

We know that many managers, however well-intentioned, will find it hard to establish the habits that seemed to come so naturally to Graham. Awareness, of course, is the first step. However, turning an awareness of the importance of inner work life into routine action takes discipline. With that in mind, we developed a checklist for managers to consult on a daily basis (see the sidebar "The Daily Progress Checklist"). The aim of the checklist is managing for meaningful progress, one day at a time.

The Progress Loop

Inner work life drives performance; in turn, good performance, which depends on consistent progress, enhances inner work life. We call this the *progress loop;* it reveals the potential for self-reinforcing benefits.

So, the most important implication of the progress principle is this: By supporting people and their daily progress in meaningful work, managers improve not only the inner work lives of their employees but also the organization's long-term performance, which enhances inner work life even more. Of course, there is a dark side—the possibility of negative feedback loops. If managers fail to support progress and the people trying to make it, inner work life suffers and so does performance; and degraded performance further undermines inner work life.

A second implication of the progress principle is that managers needn't fret about trying to read the psyches of their workers, or manipulate complicated incentive schemes, to ensure that employees are motivated and happy. As long as they show basic respect and consideration, they can focus on supporting the work itself.

To become an effective manager, you must learn to set this positive feedback loop in motion. That may require a significant shift. Business schools, business books, and managers themselves usually focus on managing organizations or people. But if you focus on managing progress, the management of people—and even of entire organizations—becomes much more feasible. You won't have to figure out how to x?ray the inner work lives of subordinates; if you facilitate their steady progress in meaningful work, make that progress salient to them, and treat them well, they will experience the emotions, motivations, and perceptions necessary for great performance. Their superior work will contribute to organizational success. And here's the beauty of it: They will love their jobs.

Originally published in May 2011. Reprint R1105C

Building the Emotional Intelligence of Groups

by Vanessa Urch Druskat and Steven B. Wolff

WHEN MANAGERS FIRST STARTED HEARING ABOUT the concept of emotional intelligence in the 1990s, scales fell from their eyes. The basic message, that effectiveness in organizations is at least as much about EQ as IQ, resonated deeply; it was something that people knew in their guts but that had never before been so well articulated. Most important, the idea held the potential for positive change. Instead of being stuck with the hand they'd been dealt, people could take steps to enhance their emotional intelligence and make themselves more effective in their work and personal lives.

Indeed, the concept of emotional intelligence had real impact. The only problem is that so far emotional intelligence has been viewed only as an individual competency, when the reality is that most work in organizations is done by teams. And if managers have one pressing need today, it's to find ways to make teams work better.

It is with real excitement, therefore, that we share these findings from our research: individual emotional intelligence has a group analog, and it is just as critical to groups' effectiveness. Teams can develop greater emotional intelligence and, in so doing, boost their overall performance.

Why Should Teams Build Their Emotional Intelligence?

No one would dispute the importance of making teams work more effectively. But most research about how to do so has focused on identifying the task processes that distinguish the most successful teams—that is, specifying the need for cooperation, participation, commitment to goals, and so forth. The assumption seems to be that, once identified, these processes can simply be imitated by other teams, with similar effect. It's not true. By analogy, think of it this way: a piano student can be taught to play Minuet in G, but he won't become a modern-day Bach without knowing music theory and being able to play with heart. Similarly, the real source of a great team's success lies in the fundamental conditions that allow effective task processes to emerge—and that cause members to engage in them wholeheartedly.

Our research tells us that three conditions are essential to a group's effectiveness: trust among members, a sense of group identity, and a sense of group efficacy. When these conditions are absent, going through the motions of cooperating and participating is still possible. But the team will not be as effective as it could be, because members will choose to hold back rather than fully engage. To be most effective, the team needs to create emotionally intelligent norms—the attitudes and behaviors that eventually become habits—that support behaviors for building trust, group identity, and group efficacy. The outcome is complete engagement in tasks. (For more on how emotional intelligence influences these conditions, see the sidebar "A Model of Team Effectiveness.")

Three Levels of Emotional Interaction

Make no mistake: a team with emotionally intelligent members does not necessarily make for an emotionally intelligent group. A team, like any social group, takes on its own character. So creating an upward, self-reinforcing spiral of trust, group identity, and group efficacy requires more than a few members who exhibit emotionally

Idea in Brief

How does IDEO, the celebrated industrial-design firm, ensure that its teams consistently produce the most innovative products under intense deadline and budget pressures? By focusing on its teams' **emotional intelligence**—that powerful combination of self-management skills and ability to relate to others.

Many executives realize that EQ (emotional quotient) is as critical as IQ to an individual's effectiveness. But *groups'* emotional intelligence may be even more important, since most work gets done in teams.

A group's EI isn't simply the sum of its members'. Instead, it comes from norms that support awareness and regulation of emotions within and outside the team. These norms build trust, group identity, and a sense of group efficacy. Members feel that they work better *together* than individually.

Group EI norms build the foundation for true collaboration and cooperation—helping otherwise skilled teams fulfill their highest potential.

intelligent behavior. It requires a team atmosphere in which the norms build emotional capacity (the ability to respond constructively in emotionally uncomfortable situations) and influence emotions in constructive ways.

Team emotional intelligence is more complicated than individual emotional intelligence because teams interact at more levels. To understand the differences, let's first look at the concept of individual emotional intelligence as defined by Daniel Goleman. In his definitive book *Emotional Intelligence,* Goleman explains the chief characteristics of someone with high EI; he or she is *aware* of emotions and able to *regulate* them—and this awareness and regulation are directed both *inward,* to one's self, and *outward,* to others. "Personal competence," in Goleman's words, comes from being aware of and regulating one's own emotions. "Social competence" is awareness and regulation of others' emotions.

A group, however, must attend to yet another level of awareness and regulation. It must be mindful of the emotions of its members,

Idea in Practice

To build a foundation for emotional intelligence, a group must be aware of and constructively regulate the emotions of:

- individual team members
- the whole group
- other key groups with whom it interacts.

How? By establishing EI norms—rules for behavior that are introduced by group leaders, training, or the larger organizational culture. Here are some examples of norms—and what they look like in action— from IDEO:

Emotions of . . .	To Hone Awareness . . .	To Regulate . . .	IDEO Examples
Individual team members	• Understand the sources of individuals' behavior and take steps to address problematic behavior. • Encourage all group members to share their perspectives before making key decisions.	• Handle confrontation constructively. If team members fall short, call them on it by letting them know the group needs them. • Treat each other in a caring way— acknowledge when someone is upset; show appreciation and respect.	• Awareness: A project leader notices a designer's frustration over a market-ing decision and initiates negotiations to resolve the issue. • Regulation: During brainstorming sessions, par-ticipants pelt colleagues with soft toys if they prematurely judge ideas.

its own group emotions or moods, and the emotions of other groups and individuals outside its boundaries.

In this article, we'll explore how emotional incompetence at any of these levels can cause dysfunction. We'll also show how establishing specific group norms that create awareness and regulation

Emotions of . . .	To Hone Awareness . . .	To Regulate . . .	IDEO Examples
The whole group	• Regularly assess the group's strengths, weaknesses, and modes of interaction. • Invite reality checks from customers, colleagues, suppliers.	• Create structures that let the group express its emotions. • Cultivate an affirmative environment. • Encourage proactive problem-solving.	• Awareness: Teams work closely with customers to determine what needs improvement. • Regulation: "Finger-blaster" toys scattered around the office let people have fun and vent stress.
Other key groups	• Designate team members as liaisons to key outside constituencies. • Identify and support other groups' expectations and needs.	• Develop cross-boundary relationships to gain outsiders' confidence. • Know the broader social and political context in which your group must succeed. • Show your appreciation of other groups.	• Regulation: IDEO built such a good relationship with an outside fabricator that it was able to call on it for help during a crisis—on the weekend.

of emotion at these three levels can lead to better outcomes. First, we'll focus on the individual level—how emotionally intelligent groups work with their individual members' emotions. Next, we'll focus on the group level. And finally, we'll look at the cross-boundary level.

A Model of Team Effectiveness

STUDY AFTER STUDY HAS shown that teams are more creative and productive when they can achieve high levels of participation, cooperation, and collaboration among members. But interactive behaviors like these aren't easy to legislate. Our work shows that three basic conditions need to be present before such behaviors can occur: mutual trust among members, a sense of group identity (a feeling among members that they belong to a unique and worthwhile group), and a sense of group efficacy (the belief that the team can perform well and that group members are more effective working together than apart).

At the heart of these three conditions are emotions. Trust, a sense of identity, and a feeling of efficacy arise in environments where emotion is well handled, so groups stand to benefit by building their emotional intelligence.

Group emotional intelligence isn't a question of dealing with a necessary evil—catching emotions as they bubble up and promptly suppressing them. Far from it. It's about bringing emotions deliberately to the surface and understanding how they affect the team's work. It's also about behaving in ways that build relationships both inside and outside the team and that strengthen the team's ability to face challenges. Emotional intelligence means exploring, embracing, and ultimately relying on emotion in work that is, at the end of the day, deeply human.

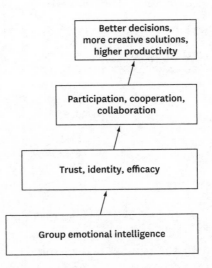

Working with Individuals' Emotions

Jill Kasper, head of her company's customer service department, is naturally tapped to join a new cross-functional team focused on enhancing the customer experience: she has extensive experience in and a real passion for customer service. But her teammates find she brings little more than a bad attitude to the table. At an early brainstorming session, Jill sits silent, arms crossed, rolling her eyes. Whenever the team starts to get energized about an idea, she launches into a detailed account of how a similar idea went nowhere in the past. The group is confused: this is the customer service star they've been hearing about? Little do they realize she feels insulted by the very formation of the team. To her, it implies she hasn't done her job well enough.

When a member is not on the same emotional wave-length as the rest, a team needs to be emotionally intelligent vis-à-vis that individual. In part, that simply means being aware of the problem. Having a norm that encourages interpersonal understanding might facilitate an awareness that Jill is acting out of defensiveness. And picking up on this defensiveness is necessary if the team wants to make her understand its desire to amplify her good work, not negate it.

Some teams seem to be able to do this naturally. At Hewlett-Packard, for instance, we learned of a team that was attempting to cross-train its members. The idea was that if each member could pinch-hit on everyone else's job, the team could deploy efforts to whatever task required the most attention. But one member seemed very uncomfortable with learning new skills and tasks; accustomed to being a top producer in his own job, he hated not knowing how to do a job perfectly. Luckily, his teammates recognized his discomfort, and rather than being annoyed, they redoubled their efforts to support him. This team benefited from a group norm it had established over time emphasizing interpersonal understanding. The norm had grown out of the group's realization that working to accurately hear and understand one another's feelings and concerns improved member morale and a willingness to cooperate.

Many teams build high emotional intelligence by taking pains to consider matters from an individual member's perspective. Think of a situation where a team of four must reach a decision; three favor one direction and the fourth favors another. In the interest of expedience, many teams in this situation would move directly to a majority vote. But a more emotionally intelligent group would pause first to hear out the objection. It would also ask if everyone were completely behind the decision, even if there appeared to be consensus. Such groups would ask, "Are there any perspectives we haven't heard yet or thought through completely?"

Perspective taking is a team behavior that teamwork experts discuss often—but not in terms of its emotional consequence. Many teams are trained to use perspective-taking techniques to make decisions or solve problems (a common tool is affinity diagramming). But these techniques may or may not improve a group's emotional intelligence. The problem is that many of these techniques consciously attempt to remove emotion from the process by collecting and combining perspectives in a mechanical way. A more effective approach to perspective taking is to ensure that team members see one another making the effort to grapple with perspectives; that way, the team has a better chance of creating the kind of trust that leads to greater participation among members.

An executive team at the Hay Group, a consulting firm, engages in the kind of deep perspective taking we're describing. The team has done role-playing exercises in which members adopt others' opinions and styles of interaction. It has also used a "storyboarding" technique, in which each member creates a small poster representing his or her ideas. As team members will attest, these methods and others have helped the group build trust and increase participation.

Regulating Individuals' Emotions

Interpersonal understanding and perspective taking are two ways that groups can become more aware of their members' perspectives and feelings. But just as important as awareness is the ability to regulate those emotions—to have a positive impact on how they are expressed and even on how individual team members feel. We're not talking about imposing groupthink or some other form of manipulation here—clearly, the goal must be to balance the team's cohesion with members' individuality. We're simply acknowledging that people take their emotional cues from those around them. Something that seems upsetting initially can seem not so bad—or ten times worse—depending on whether one's colleagues are inclined to smooth feathers or fan flames. The most constructive way of regulating team members' emotions is by establishing norms in the group for both confrontation and caring.

It may seem illogical to suggest that an emotionally intelligent group must engage in confrontation, but it's not. Inevitably, a team member will indulge in behavior that crosses the line, and the team must feel comfortable calling the foul. In one manufacturing team we studied, a member told us about the day she selfishly decided to extend her break. Before long, one of her teammates stormed into the break room, saying, "What are you doing in here? Get back out on the floor—your team needs you!" The woman had overstepped the bounds, and she got called on it. There were no hard feelings, because the woman knew the group valued her contributions.

Some teams also find that a little humor helps when pointing out errant behavior. Teasing someone who is habitually late for meetings, for instance, can make that person aware of how important timeliness is to the group. Done right, confrontation can be seen in a positive light; it's a way for the group to say, "We want you in—we need your contribution." And it's especially important when a team must work together on a long-term assignment. Without confrontation, disruptive behavior can fester and erode a sense of trust in a team.

Establishing norms that reinforce caring behavior is often not very difficult and usually a matter of concentrating on little things. When an individual is upset, for example, it may make all the difference to have group members acknowledge that person's feelings. We saw this in a meeting where one team member arrived angry because the time and place of the meeting was very inconvenient for him. When another member announced the sacrifice the man had made to be there, and thanked him, the man's attitude turned around 180 degrees. In general, a caring orientation includes displaying positive regard, appreciation, and respect for group members through behaviors such as support, validation, and compassion.

Interpersonal understanding, perspective taking, confrontation, caring—these norms build trust and a sense of group identity among members. And all of them can be established in teams where they don't arise naturally. You may ask, But is it really worth all the effort? Does it make sense to spend managerial time fostering new norms to accommodate a few prickly personalities? Of course it does. Teams are at the very foundation of an organization, and they won't work effectively without mutual trust and a common commitment to goals.

Working with Group Emotions

Chris couldn't believe it, but he was requesting a reassignment. The team he was on was doing good work, staying on budget, and hitting all its deadlines—though not always elegantly. Its leader, Stan Evans, just got a promotion. So why was being on the team such a downer? At the last major status meeting, they should have been serving champagne—so much had been achieved. Instead, everyone was thoroughly dispirited over a setback they hadn't foreseen, which turned out later to be no big deal. It seemed no matter what happened, the group griped. The team even saw Stan's promotion in a negative light: "Oh, so I guess management wants to keep a closer eye on us" and "I hear Stan's new boss doesn't back this project." Chris had a friend on another team who was happy to put in a good word for him. The work was inherently less interesting—but hey, at least they were having fun.

———————

Some teams suffer because they aren't aware of emotions at the group level. Chris's team, for instance, isn't aware of all it has achieved, and it doesn't acknowledge that it has fallen into a malaise. In our study of effective teams, we've found that having norms for group self-awareness—of emotional states, strengths and weaknesses, modes of interaction, and task processes—is a critical part of group emotional intelligence that facilitates group efficacy. Teams gain it both through self-evaluation and by soliciting feedback from others.

Self-evaluation can take the form of a formal event or a constant activity. At Sherwin Williams, a group of managers was starting a new initiative that would require higher levels of teamwork. Group members hired a consultant, but before the consultant arrived, they met to assess their strengths and weaknesses as a team. They found that merely articulating the issues was an important step toward building their capabilities.

A far less formal method of raising group emotional awareness is through the kind of activity we saw at the Veterans Health Administration's Center for Leadership and Development. Managers there have developed a norm in which they are encouraged to speak up when they feel the group is not being productive. For example, if there's a post-lunch lull and people on the team are low on energy, someone might say, "Don't we look like a bunch of sad sacks?" With attention called to it, the group makes an effort to refocus.

Emotionally competent teams don't wear blinders; they have the emotional capacity to face potentially difficult information and actively seek opinions on their task processes, progress, and performance from the outside. For some teams, feedback may come directly from customers. Others look to colleagues within the company, to suppliers, or to professional peers. A group of designers we studied routinely posts its work in progress on walls throughout the building, with invitations to comment and critique. Similarly, many advertising agencies see annual industry competitions as a valuable source of feedback on their creative teams' work.

Regulating Group Emotions

Many teams make conscious efforts to build team spirit. Team-building outings, whether purely social or Outward Bound—style physical challenges, are popular methods for building this sense of collective enthusiasm. What's going on here is that teams and their leaders recognize they can improve a team's overall attitude—that is, they are regulating group-level emotion. And while the focus of a team-building exercise is often not directly related to a group's actual work, the benefits are highly relevant: teams come away with higher emotional capacity and thus a greater ability to respond to emotional challenges.

The most effective teams we have studied go far beyond the occasional "ropes and rocks" off-site. They have established norms that strengthen their ability to respond effectively to the kind of emotional challenges a group confronts on a daily basis. The norms they favor accomplish three main things: they create resources for working with emotions, foster an affirmative environment, and encourage proactive problem solving.

Teams need resources that all members can draw on to deal with group emotions. One important resource is a common vocabulary. To use an example, a group member at the Veterans Health Administration picked up on another member's bad mood and told him that he was just "cranky" today. The "cranky" term stuck and became the group's gentle way of letting someone know that their negativity was having a bad effect on the group. Other resources may include helpful ways to vent frustrations. One executive team leader we interviewed described his team's practice of making time for a "wailing wall"—a few minutes of whining and moaning about some setback. Releasing and acknowledging those negative emotions, the leader says, allows the group to refocus its attention on the parts of the situation it can control and channel its energy in a positive direction. But sometimes, venting takes more than words. We've seen more than one intense workplace outfitted with toys—like soft projectile shooters—that have been used in games of cube warfare.

Perhaps the most obvious way to build emotional capacity through regulating team-level emotion is simply to create an affirmative environment. Everyone values a team that, when faced with a challenge, responds with a can-do attitude. Again, it's a question of having the right group norms—in this case, favoring optimism, and positive images and interpretations over negative ones. This doesn't always come naturally to a team, as one executive we interviewed at the Hay Group knows. When external conditions create a cycle of negativity among group members, he takes it upon himself to change the atmosphere of the group. He consciously resists the temptation to join the complaining and blaming and instead tries to reverse the cycle with a positive, constructive note.

One of the most powerful norms we have seen for building a group's ability to respond to emotionally challenging situations is an emphasis on proactive problem solving. We saw a lot of this going on in a manufacturing team we observed at AMP Corporation. Much of what this team needed to hit its targets was out of its strict control. But rather than sit back and point fingers, the team worked hard to get what it needed from others, and in some cases, took matters into its own hands. In one instance, an alignment problem in a key machine was creating faulty products. The team studied the problem and approached the engineering group with its own suggested design for a part that might correct the problem. The device worked, and the number of defective products decreased significantly.

This kind of problem solving is valuable for many reasons. It obviously serves the company by removing one more obstacle to profitability. But, to the point of our work, it also shows a team in control of its own emotions. It refused to feel powerless and was eager to take charge.

Working with Emotions Outside the Group

Jim sighed. The "Bugs" team was at it again. Didn't they see that while they were high-fiving one another over their impressive productivity, the rest of the organization was paying for it? This time, in their self-managed wisdom, they'd decided to make a three months' supply of one component. No changeover meant no machine downtime and a record low cost per unit. But now the group downstream was swamped with inventory it didn't need and worried about shortages of something else. Jim braced himself for his visit to the floor. The Bugs didn't take criticism well; they seemed to think they were flawless and that everyone else was just trying to take them down a notch. And what was with that name, anyway? Some kind of inside joke, Jim guessed. Too bad nobody else got it.

The last kind of emotional intelligence any high-performing team should have relates to cross-boundary relationships. Just as individuals should be mindful of their own emotions and others', groups should look both inward and outward emotionally. In the case of the Bugs, the team is acting like a clique—creating close emotional ties within but ignoring the feelings, needs, and concerns of important individuals and teams in the broader organization.

Some teams have developed norms that are particularly helpful in making them aware of the broader organizational context. One practice is to have various team members act as liaisons to important constituencies. Many teams are already made up of members drawn from different parts of an organization, so a cross-boundary perspective comes naturally. Others need to work a little harder. One team we studied realized it would be important to understand the perspective of its labor union. Consequently, a team member from HR went to some lengths to discover the right channels for having a union member appointed to the group. A cross-boundary perspective is especially important in situations where a team's work will have significant impact on others in the organization—for example, where a team is asked to design an intranet to serve everyone's needs. We've seen many situations in which a team is so enamored of its solution that it is caught completely by surprise when others in the company don't share its enthusiasm.

Some of the most emotionally intelligent teams we have seen are so attuned to their broader organizational context that it affects how they frame and communicate their own needs and accomplishments. A team at the chemical-processing company KoSa, for example, felt it needed a new piece of manufacturing equipment, but senior management wasn't so sure the purchase was a priority. Aware that the decision makers were still on the fence, the team decided to emphasize the employee safety benefits of the new machine—just one aspect of its desirability to them, but an issue of paramount importance to management. At a plant safety meeting attended by high-level managers, they made the case that the equipment they were seeking would greatly reduce the risk of injury to workers. A few weeks later they got it.

Sometimes, a team must be particularly aware of the needs and feelings of another group within the organization. We worked with an information technology company where the hardware engineers worked separately from the software engineers to achieve the same goal—faster processing and fewer crashes. Each could achieve only so much independently. When finally a hardware team leader went out of his way to build relationships with the software people, the two teams began to cooperate—and together, they achieved 20% to 40% higher performance than had been targeted.

This kind of positive outcome can be facilitated by norms that encourage a group to recognize the feelings and needs of other groups. We saw effective norms for interteam awareness at a division of AMP, where each manufacturing team is responsible for a step in the manufacturing process and they need one another to complete the product on time. Team leaders there meet in the morning to understand the needs, resources, and schedules of each team. If one team is ahead and another is behind, they reallocate resources. Members of the faster

Building Norms for Three Levels of Group Emotional Intelligence

GROUP EMOTIONAL INTELLIGENCE IS about the small acts that make a big difference. It is not about a team member working all night to meet a deadline; it is about saying thank you for doing so. It is not about in-depth discussion of ideas; it is about asking a quiet member for his thoughts. It is not about harmony, lack of tension, and all members liking each other; it is about acknowledging when harmony is false, tension is unexpressed, and treating others with respect. The following table outlines some of the small things that groups can do to establish the norms that build group emotional intelligence.

Norms that create awareness of emotions

Individual	Group	Cross-boundary
Interpersonal understanding	**Team self-evaluation**	**Organizational understanding**
1. Take time away from group tasks to get to know one another.	1. Schedule time to examine team effectiveness.	1. Find out the concerns and needs of others in the organization.
2. Have a "check in" at the beginning of the meeting—that is, ask how everyone is doing.	2. Create measurable task and process objectives and then measure them.	2. Consider who can influence the team's ability to accomplish its goals.
3. Assume that undesirable behavior takes place for a reason. Find out what that reason is. Ask questions and listen. Avoid negative attributions.	3. Acknowledge and discuss group moods.	3. Discuss the culture and politics in the organization.
4. Tell your teammates what you're thinking and how you're feeling.	4. Communicate your sense of what is transpiring in the team.	4. Ask whether proposed team actions are congruent with the organization's culture and politics.
	5. Allow members to call a "process check." (For instance, a team member might say, "Process check: is this the most effective use of our time right now?")	
Perspective taking	**Seeking feedback**	
1. Ask whether everyone agrees with a decision.	1. Ask your "customers" how you are doing.	
2. Ask quiet members what they think.	2. Post your work and invite comments.	
3. Question decisions that come too quickly.	3. Benchmark your processes.	
4. Appoint a devil's advocate.		

Norms that help regulate emotions

Confronting

1. Set ground rules and use them to point out errant behavior.
2. Call members on errant behavior.
3. Create playful devices for pointing out such behavior. These often emerge from the group spontaneously. Reinforce them.

Caring

1. Support members: volunteer to help them if they need it, be flexible, and provide emotional support.
2. Validate members' contributions. Let members know they are valued.
3. Protect members from attack.
4. Respect individuality and differences in perspectives. Listen.
5. Never be derogatory or demeaning.

Creating resources for working with emotion

1. Make time to discuss difficult issues, and address the emotions that surround them.
2. Find creative, shorthand ways to acknowledge and express the emotion in the group.
3. Create fun ways to acknowledge and relieve stress and tension.
4. Express acceptance of members' emotions.

Creating an affirmative environment

1. Reinforce that the team can meet a challenge. Be optimistic. For example, say things like, "We can get through this" or "Nothing will stop us."
2. Focus on what you can control.
3. Remind members of the group's important and positive mission.
4. Remind the group how it solved a similar problem before.
5. Focus on problem solving, not blaming.

Solving problems proactively

1. Anticipate problems and address them before they happen.
2. Take the initiative to understand and get what you need to be effective.
3. Do it yourself if others aren't responding. Rely on yourself, not others.

Building external relationships

1. Create opportunities for networking and interaction.
2. Ask about the needs of other teams.
3. Provide support for other teams.
4. Invite others to team meetings if they might have a stake in what you are doing.

team help the team that's behind and do so in a friendly way that empathizes with their situation and builds the relationship.

Most of the examples we've been citing show teams that are not only aware of but also able to influence outsiders' needs and perspectives. This ability to regulate emotion at the cross-boundary level is a group's version of the "social skills" so critical to individual emotional intelligence. It involves developing external relationships and gaining the confidence of outsiders, adopting an ambassadorial role instead of an isolationist one.

A manufacturing team we saw at KoSa displayed very high social skills in working with its maintenance team. It recognized that, when problems occurred in the plant, the maintenance team often had many activities on its plate. All things being equal, what would make the maintenance team consider this particular manufacturing group a high priority? Knowing a good relationship would be a factor, the manufacturing team worked hard to build good ties with the maintenance people. At one point, for instance, the manufacturing team showed its appreciation by nominating the maintenance team for "Team of the Quarter" recognition—and then doing all the letter writing and behind-the-scenes praising that would ultimately help the maintenance team win. In turn, the manufacturing team's good relationship with maintenance helped it become one of the highest producers in the plant.

A Model for Group Emotional Intelligence

We've been discussing the need for teams to learn to channel emotion effectively at the three levels of human interaction important to them: team to individual member, team to itself, and team to outside entities. Together, the norms we've been exploring help groups work with emotions productively and intelligently. Often, groups with emotionally intelligent members have norms like these in place, but it's unlikely any group would unconsciously come up with *all* the norms we have outlined. In other words, this is a model for group emotional intelligence that any work team could benefit from by applying it deliberately.

What would the ultimate emotionally intelligent team look like? Closest to the ideal are some of the teams we've seen at IDEO, the celebrated industrial design firm. IDEO's creative teams are responsible for the look and feel of products like Apple's first mouse, the Crest toothpaste tube, and the Palm V personal digital assistant. The firm routinely wins competitions for the form and function of its designs and even has a business that teaches creative problem-solving techniques to other companies.

The nature of IDEO's work calls for high group emotional intelligence. Under pressure of client deadlines and budget estimates, the company must deliver innovative, aesthetic solutions that balance human needs with engineering realities. It's a deep philosophical belief at IDEO that great design is best accomplished through the creative friction of diverse teams and not the solitary pursuit of brilliant individuals, so it's imperative that the teams at IDEO click. In our study of those teams, we found group norms supporting emotional intelligence at all three levels of our model.

First, the teams at IDEO are very aware of individual team members' emotions, and they are adept at regulating them. For example, an IDEO designer became very frustrated because someone from marketing was insisting a logo be applied to the designer's product, which he felt would ruin it visually. At a meeting about the product, the team's project leader picked up on the fact that something was wrong. The designer was sitting off by himself, and things "didn't look right." The project leader looked into the situation and then initiated a negotiation that led to a mutual solution.

IDEO team members also confront one another when they break norms. This is common during brainstorming sessions, where the rule is that people must defer judgment and avoid shooting down ideas. If someone breaks that norm, the team comes down on him in a playful yet forceful way (imagine being pelted by foam toys). Or if someone is out of line, the norm is to stand up and call her on it immediately. If a client is in the room, the confrontation is subtler— perhaps a kick under the chair.

Teams at IDEO also demonstrate strengths in group-focused emotional intelligence. To ensure they have a high level of self-awareness, teams constantly seek feedback from both inside and outside the organization. Most important, they work very closely with customers. If a design is not meeting customer expectations, the team finds out quickly and takes steps to modify it.

Regulating group emotion at IDEO often means providing outlets for stress. This is a company that believes in playing and having fun. Several hundred finger blasters (a toy that shoots soft projectiles) have been placed around the building for employees to pick up and start shooting when they're frustrated. Indeed, the design firm's culture welcomes the expression of emotions, so it's not uncommon for someone—whether happy or angry — to stand up and yell. IDEO has even created fun office projects that people can work on if they need a break. For example, they might have a project to design the company holiday card or to design the "tourist stop" displays seen by visitors.

Finally, IDEO teams also have norms to ensure they are aware of the needs and concerns of people outside their boundaries and that they use that awareness to develop relationships with those individuals and groups. On display at IDEO is a curious model: a toy truck with plastic pieces on springs that pop out of the bed of the truck when a button is pressed. It turns out the model commemorates an incident that taught a variety of lessons. The story centers on a design team that had been working for three weeks on a very complex plastic enclosure for a product. Unfortunately, on the Thursday before a Monday client deadline, when an engineer was taking it to be painted, it slipped from his pickup bed and exploded on the road at 70 mph. The team was willing to work through the weekend to rebuild the part but couldn't finish it without the help of the outside fabricator it had used on the original. Because they had taken the time to build a good relationship with the fabricator, its people were willing to go above and beyond the call of duty. The light-hearted display was a way for teammates to show the engineer that all was forgiven—and a reminder to the rest of the organization of how a team in crisis can get by with a little help from its friends.

Where Do Norms Come From?

Not every company is as dependent on teams and their emotional intelligence as IDEO. But now more than ever, we see companies depending on teams for decisions and tasks that, in another time, would have been the work of individuals. And unfortunately, we also see them discovering that a team can have everything going for it—the brightest and most qualified people, access to resources, a clear mission—but still fail because it lacks group emotional intelligence.

Norms that build trust, group identity, and group efficacy are the key to making teams click. They allow an otherwise highly skilled and resourced team to fulfill its potential, and they can help a team faced with substantial challenges achieve surprising victories. So how do norms as powerful as the ones we've described in this article come about? In our research, we saw them being introduced from any of five basic directions: by formal team leaders, by informal team leaders, by courageous followers, through training, or from the larger organizational culture. (For more on how to establish the norms described in this article, see the sidebar "Building Norms for Three Levels of Group Emotional Intelligence.")

At the Hay Group, for example, it was the deliberate action of a team leader that helped one group see the importance of emotions to the group's overall effectiveness. Because this particular group was composed of managers from many different cultures, its leader knew he couldn't assume all the members possessed a high level of interpersonal understanding. To establish that norm, he introduced novelties like having a meeting without a table, using smaller groups, and conducting an inventory of team members' various learning styles.

Interventions like these can probably be done only by a formal team leader. The ways informal leaders or other team members enhance emotional intelligence are typically more subtle, though often just as powerful. Anyone might advance the cause, for example, by speaking up if the group appears to be ignoring an important perspective or feeling—or simply by doing his or her part to create an affirmative environment.

Training courses can also go a long way toward increasing emotional awareness and showing people how to regulate emotions. We know of many companies that now focus on emotional issues in leadership development courses, negotiation and communication workshops, and employee-assistance programs like those for stress management. These training programs can sensitize team members to the importance of establishing emotionally intelligent norms.

Finally, perhaps more than anything, a team can be influenced by a broader organizational culture that recognizes and celebrates employee emotion. This is clearly the case at IDEO and, we believe, at many of the companies creating the greatest value in the new economy. Unfortunately, it's the most difficult piece of the puzzle to put in place at companies that don't already have it. For organizations with long histories of employees checking their emotions at the door, change will occur, if at all, one team at a time.

Becoming Intelligent About Emotion

The research presented in this article arose from one simple imperative: in an era of teamwork, it's essential to figure out what makes teams work. Our research shows that, just like individuals, the most effective teams are emotionally intelligent ones—and that any team can attain emotional intelligence.

In this article, we've attempted to lay out a model for positive change, containing the most important types of norms a group can create to enhance its emotional intelligence. Teams, like all groups, operate according to such norms. By working to establish norms for emotional awareness and regulation at all levels of interaction, teams can build the solid foundation of trust, group identity, and group efficacy they need for true cooperation and collaboration—and high performance overall.

Originally published in March 2001. Reprint 620X

Managing Multicultural Teams

by Jeanne Brett, Kristin Behfar, and Mary C. Kern

WHEN A MAJOR INTERNATIONAL SOFTWARE developer needed to produce a new product quickly, the project manager assembled a team of employees from India and the United States. From the start the team members could not agree on a delivery date for the product. The Americans thought the work could be done in two to three weeks; the Indians predicted it would take two to three months. As time went on, the Indian team members proved reluctant to report setbacks in the production process, which the American team members would find out about only when work was due to be passed to them. Such conflicts, of course, may affect any team, but in this case they arose from cultural differences. As tensions mounted, conflict over delivery dates and feedback became personal, disrupting team members' communication about even mundane issues. The project manager decided he had to intervene—with the result that both the American and the Indian team members came to rely on him for direction regarding minute operational details that the team should have been able to handle itself. The manager became so bogged down by quotidian issues that the project careened hopelessly off even the most pessimistic schedule—and the team never learned to work together effectively.

Multicultural teams often generate frustrating management dilemmas. Cultural differences can create substantial obstacles to effective teamwork—but these may be subtle and difficult to recognize until significant damage has already been done. As in the case above, which the manager involved told us about, managers may create more problems than they resolve by intervening. The challenge in managing multicultural teams effectively is to recognize underlying cultural causes of conflict, and to intervene in ways that both get the team back on track and empower its members to deal with future challenges themselves.

We interviewed managers and members of multicultural teams from all over the world. These interviews, combined with our deep research on dispute resolution and teamwork, led us to conclude that the wrong kind of managerial intervention may sideline valuable members who should be participating or, worse, create resistance, resulting in poor team performance. We're not talking here about respecting differing national standards for doing business, such as accounting practices. We're referring to day-to-day working problems among team members that can keep multicultural teams from realizing the very gains they were set up to harvest, such as knowledge of different product markets, culturally sensitive customer service, and 24-hour work rotations.

The good news is that cultural challenges are manageable if managers and team members choose the right strategy and avoid imposing single-culture-based approaches on multicultural situations.

The Challenges

People tend to assume that challenges on multicultural teams arise from differing styles of communication. But this is only one of the four categories that, according to our research, can create barriers to a team's ultimate success. These categories are direct versus indirect communication; trouble with accents and fluency; differing attitudes toward hierarchy and authority; and conflicting norms for decision making.

Direct versus indirect communication

Communication in Western cultures is typically direct and explicit. The meaning is on the surface, and a listener doesn't have to know

Idea in Brief

If your company does business internationally, you're probably leading teams with members from diverse cultural backgrounds. Those differences can present serious obstacles. For example, some members' lack of fluency in the team's dominant language can lead others to underestimate their competence. When such obstacles arise, your team can stalemate.

To get the team moving again, avoid intervening directly, advise Brett, Behfar, and Kern. Though sometimes necessary, your involvement can prevent team members from solving problems themselves—and learning from that process.

Instead, choose one of three indirect interventions. When possible, encourage team members to **adapt** by acknowledging cultural gaps and working around them. If your team isn't able to be open about their differences, consider **structural intervention** (e.g., reassigning members to reduce interpersonal friction). As a last resort, use an **exit** strategy (e.g., removing a member from the team).

There's no one right way to tackle multicultural problems. But understanding four barriers to team success can help you begin evaluating possible responses.

much about the context or the speaker to interpret it. This is not true in many other cultures, where meaning is embedded in the way the message is presented. For example, Western negotiators get crucial information about the other party's preferences and priorities by asking direct questions, such as "Do you prefer option A or option B?" In cultures that use indirect communication, negotiators may have to infer preferences and priorities from changes—or the lack of them— in the other party's settlement proposal. In cross-cultural negotiations, the non-Westerner can understand the direct communications of the Westerner, but the Westerner has difficulty understanding the indirect communications of the non-Westerner.

An American manager who was leading a project to build an interface for a U.S. and Japanese customer-data system explained the problems her team was having this way: "In Japan, they want to talk and discuss. Then we take a break and they talk within the organization. They want to make sure that there's harmony in the rest of the organization. One of the hardest lessons for me was when I thought they were saying yes but they just meant 'I'm listening to you.'"

Idea in Practice

Four Barriers

The following cultural differences can cause destructive conflicts in a team:

- **Direct versus indirect communication.** Some team members use direct, explicit communication while others are indirect, for example, asking questions instead of pointing out problems with a project. When members see such differences as violations of their culture's communication norms, relationships can suffer.

- **Trouble with accents and fluency.** Members who aren't fluent in the team's dominant language may have difficulty communicating their knowledge. This can prevent the team from using their expertise and create frustration or perceptions of incompetence.

- **Differing attitudes toward hierarchy.** Team members from hierarchical cultures expect to be treated differently according to their status in the organization. Members from egalitarian cultures do not. Failure of some members to honor those expectations can cause humiliation or loss of stature and credibility.

- **Conflicting decision-making norms.** Members vary in how quickly they make decisions and in how much analysis they require beforehand. Someone who prefers making decisions quickly may grow frustrated with those who need more time.

Four Interventions

Your team's unique circumstances can help you determine how to respond to multicultural conflicts. Consider these options:

Intervention Type	When to Use	Example
Adaptation: working with or around differences	Members are willing to acknowledge cultural differences and figure out how to live with them.	An American engineer working on a team that included Israelis was shocked by their in-your-face, argumentative style. Once he noticed they confronted each other and not just

Intervention Type	When to Use	Example
		him—and still worked well together—he realized confrontations weren't personal attacks and accepted their style.
Structural intervention: reorganizing to reduce friction	The team has obvious subgroups, or members cling to negative stereotypes of one another.	An international research team's leader realized that when he led meetings, members "shut down" because they felt intimidated by his executive status. After he hired a consultant to run future meetings, members participated more.
Managerial intervention: making final decisions without team involvement	Rarely; for instance, a new team needs guidance in establishing productive norms.	A software development team's lingua franca was English, but some members spoke with pronounced accents. The manager explained they'd been chosen for their task expertise, not fluency in English. And she directed them to tell customers: "I realize I have an accent. If you don't understand what I'm saying, just stop me and ask questions."
Exit: voluntary or involuntary removal of a team member	Emotions are running high, and too much face has been lost on both sides to salvage the situation.	When two members of a multicultural consulting team couldn't resolve their disagreement over how to approach problems, one member left the firm.

The differences between direct and indirect communication can cause serious damage to relationships when team projects run into problems. When the American manager quoted above discovered that several flaws in the system would significantly disrupt company operations, she pointed this out in an e-mail to her American boss and the Japanese team members. Her boss appreciated the direct warnings; her Japanese colleagues were embarrassed, because she had violated their norms for uncovering and discussing problems. Their reaction was to provide her with less access to the people and information she needed to monitor progress. They would probably have responded better if she had pointed out the problems indirectly—for example, by asking them what would happen if a certain part of the system was not functioning properly, even though she knew full well that it was malfunctioning and also what the implications were.

As our research indicates is so often true, communication challenges create barriers to effective teamwork by reducing information sharing, creating interpersonal conflict, or both. In Japan, a typical response to direct confrontation is to isolate the norm violator. This American manager was isolated not just socially but also physically. She told us, "They literally put my office in a storage room, where I had desks stacked from floor to ceiling and I was the only person there. So they totally isolated me, which was a pretty loud signal to me that I was not a part of the inside circle and that they would communicate with me only as needed."

Her direct approach had been intended to solve a problem, and in one sense, it did, because her project was launched problem-free. But her norm violations exacerbated the challenges of working with her Japanese colleagues and limited her ability to uncover any other problems that might have derailed the project later on.

Trouble with accents and fluency

Although the language of international business is English, misunderstandings or deep frustration may occur because of nonnative speakers' accents, lack of fluency, or problems with translation or usage. These may also influence perceptions of status or competence.

For example, a Latin American member of a multicultural consulting team lamented, "Many times I felt that because of the language difference, I didn't have the words to say some things that I was thinking. I noticed that when I went to these interviews with the U.S. guy, he would tend to lead the interviews, which was understandable but also disappointing, because we are at the same level. I had very good questions, but he would take the lead."

When we interviewed an American member of a U.S.-Japanese team that was assessing the potential expansion of a U.S. retail chain into Japan, she described one American teammate this way: "He was not interested in the Japanese consultants' feedback and felt that because they weren't as fluent as he was, they weren't intelligent enough and, therefore, could add no value." The team member described was responsible for assessing one aspect of the feasibility of expansion into Japan. Without input from the Japanese experts, he risked overestimating opportunities and underestimating challenges.

Nonfluent team members may well be the most expert on the team, but their difficulty communicating knowledge makes it hard for the team to recognize and utilize their expertise. If teammates become frustrated or impatient with a lack of fluency, interpersonal conflicts can arise. Nonnative speakers may become less motivated to contribute, or anxious about their performance evaluations and future career prospects. The organization as a whole pays a greater price: Its investment in a multicultural team fails to pay off.

Some teams, we learned, use language differences to resolve (rather than create) tensions. A team of U.S. and Latin American buyers was negotiating with a team from a Korean supplier. The negotiations took place in Korea, but the discussions were conducted in English. Frequently the Koreans would caucus at the table by speaking Korean. The buyers, frustrated, would respond by appearing to caucus in Spanish—though they discussed only inconsequential current events and sports, in case any of the Koreans spoke Spanish. Members of the team who didn't speak Spanish pretended to participate, to the great amusement of their teammates.

This approach proved effective: It conveyed to the Koreans in an appropriately indirect way that their caucuses in Korean were frustrating and annoying to the other side. As a result, both teams cut back on sidebar conversations.

Differing attitudes toward hierarchy and authority

A challenge inherent in multicultural teammates is that by design, teams have a rather flat structure. But team members from some cultures, in which people are treated differently according to their status in an organization, are uncomfortable on flat teams. If they defer to higher-status team members, their behavior will be seen as appropriate when most of the team comes from a hierarchical culture; but they may damage their stature and credibility—and even face humiliation—if most of the team comes from an egalitarian culture.

One manager of Mexican heritage, who was working on a credit and underwriting team for a bank, told us, "In Mexican culture, you're always supposed to be humble. So whether you understand something or not, you're supposed to put it in the form of a question. You have to keep it open-ended, out of respect. I think that actually worked against me, because the Americans thought I really didn't know what I was talking about. So it made me feel like they thought I was wavering on my answer."

When, as a result of differing cultural norms, team members believe they've been treated disrespectfully, the whole project can blow up. In another Korean-U.S. negotiation, the American members of a due diligence team were having difficulty getting information from their Korean counterparts, so they complained directly to higher-level Korean management, nearly wrecking the deal. The higher-level managers were offended because hierarchy is strictly adhered to in Korean organizations and culture. It should have been their own lower-level people, not the U.S. team members, who came to them with a problem. And the Korean team members were mortified that their bosses had been involved before they themselves could brief them. The crisis was resolved only when high-level U.S. managers made a trip to Korea, conveying appropriate respect for their Korean counterparts.

Conflicting norms for decision making

Cultures differ enormously when it comes to decision making—particularly, how quickly decisions should be made and how much analysis is required beforehand. Not surprisingly, U.S. managers like to make decisions very quickly and with relatively little analysis by comparison with managers from other countries.

A Brazilian manager at an American company who was negotiating to buy Korean products destined for Latin America told us, "On the first day, we agreed on three points, and on the second day, the U.S.-Spanish side wanted to start with point four. But the Korean side wanted to go back and rediscuss points one through three. My boss almost had an attack."

What U.S. team members learn from an experience like this is that the American way simply cannot be imposed on other cultures. Managers from other cultures may, for example, decline to share information until they understand the full scope of a project. But they have learned that they can't simply ignore the desire of their American counterparts to make decisions quickly. What to do? The best solution seems to be to make minor concessions on process—to learn to adjust to and even respect another approach to decision making. For example, American managers have learned to keep their impatient bosses away from team meetings and give them frequent if brief updates. A comparable lesson for managers from other cultures is to be explicit about what they need—saying, for example, "We have to see the big picture before we talk details."

Four Strategies

The most successful teams and managers we interviewed used four strategies for dealing with these challenges: adaptation (acknowledging cultural gaps openly and working around them), structural intervention (changing the shape of the team), managerial intervention (setting norms early or bringing in a higher-level manager), and exit (removing a team member when other options have failed). There is no one right way to deal with a particular kind of multicultural problem; identifying the type of challenge is only the first step. The more crucial step is assessing the circumstances—or "enabling situational conditions"—under which the team is working. For example, does the project allow any flexibility for change, or do deadlines make that impossible? Are there additional resources available that might be tapped? Is the team permanent or temporary? Does the team's manager have the autonomy to make a decision about changing the team in some way? Once the situational conditions have been analyzed, the team's leader can identify an appropriate response (see the exhibit "Identifying the right strategy").

Identifying the right strategy

The most successful teams and managers we interviewed use four strategies for dealing with problems: adaptation (acknowledging cultural gaps openly and working around them), structural intervention (changing the shape of the team), managerial intervention (setting norms early or bringing in a higher-level manager), and exit (removing a team member when other options have failed). Adaptation is the ideal strategy because the team works effectively to solve its own problem with minimal input from management— and, most important, learns from the experience. The guide below can help you identify the right strategy once you have identified both the problem and the "enabling situational conditions" that apply to the team.

Representative problems	Enabling situational conditions	Strategy	Complicating factors
• Conflict arises from decision-making differences • Misunderstanding or stonewalling arises from communication differences	• Team members can attribute a challenge to culture rather than personality • Higher-level managers are not available or the team would be embarrassed to involve them	Adaptation	• Team members must be exceptionally aware • Negotiating a common understanding takes time

Representative problems	Enabling situational conditions	Strategy	Complicating factors
• The team is affected by emotional tensions relating to fluency issues or prejudice • Team members are inhibited by perceived status differences among teammates	• The team can be subdivided to mix cultures or expertise • Tasks can be subdivided	Structural Intervention	• If team members aren't carefully distributed, subgroups can strengthen preexisting differences • Subgroup solutions have to fit back together
• Violations of hierarchy have resulted in loss of face • An absence of ground rules is causing conflict	• The problem has produced a high level of emotion • The team has reached a stalemate • A higher-level manager is able and willing to intervene	Managerial Intervention	• The team becomes overly dependent on the manager • Team members may be sidelined or resistant
• A team member cannot adjust to the challenge at hand and has become unable to contribute to the project	• The team is permanent rather than temporary • Emotions are beyond the point of intervention • Too much face has been lost	Exit	• Talent and training costs are lost

Adaptation

Some teams find ways to work with or around the challenges they face, adapting practices or attitudes without making changes to the group's membership or assignments. Adaptation works when team members are willing to acknowledge and name their cultural differences and to assume responsibility for figuring out how to live with them. It's often the best possible approach to a problem, because it typically involves less managerial time than other strategies; and because team members participate in solving the problem themselves, they learn from the process. When team members have this mind-set, they can be creative about protecting their own substantive differences while acceding to the processes of others.

An American software engineer located in Ireland who was working with an Israeli account management team from his own company told us how shocked he was by the Israelis' in-your-face style: "There were definitely different ways of approaching issues and discussing them. There is something pretty common to the Israeli culture: They like to argue. I tend to try to collaborate more, and it got very stressful for me until I figured out how to kind of merge the cultures."

The software engineer adapted. He imposed some structure on the Israelis that helped him maintain his own style of being thoroughly prepared; that accommodation enabled him to accept the Israeli style. He also noticed that team members weren't just confronting him; they confronted one another but were able to work together effectively nevertheless. He realized that the confrontation was not personal but cultural.

In another example, an American member of a postmerger consulting team was frustrated by the hierarchy of the French company his team was working with. He felt that a meeting with certain French managers who were not directly involved in the merger "wouldn't deliver any value to me or for purposes of the project," but said that he had come to understand that "it was very important to really involve all the people there" if the integration was ultimately to work.

A U.S. and UK multicultural team tried to use their differing approaches to decision making to reach a higher-quality decision. This approach, called fusion, is getting serious attention from political scientists and from government officials dealing with multicultural populations that want to protect their cultures rather than integrate or assimilate. If the team had relied exclusively on the Americans' "forge ahead" approach, it might not have recognized the pitfalls that lay ahead and might later have had to back up and start over. Meanwhile, the UK members would have been gritting their teeth and saying "We told you things were moving too fast." If the team had used the "Let's think about this" UK approach, it might have wasted a lot of time trying to identify every pitfall, including the most unlikely, while the U.S. members chomped at the bit and muttered about analysis paralysis. The strength of this team was that some of its members were willing to forge ahead and some were willing to work through pitfalls. To accommodate them all, the team did both—moving not quite as fast as the U.S. members would have on their own and not quite as thoroughly as the UK members would have.

Structural intervention

A structural intervention is a deliberate reorganization or reassignment designed to reduce interpersonal friction or to remove a source of conflict for one or more groups. This approach can be extremely effective when obvious subgroups demarcate the team (for example, headquarters versus national subsidiaries) or if team members are proud, defensive, threatened, or clinging to negative stereotypes of one another.

A member of an investment research team scattered across continental Europe, the UK, and the U.S. described for us how his manager resolved conflicts stemming from status differences and language tensions among the team's three "tribes." The manager started by having the team meet face-to-face twice a year, not to discuss mundane day-to-day problems (of which there were many) but to identify a set of values that the team would use to direct and evaluate its progress. At the first meeting, he realized that when he started to speak, everyone else "shut down," waiting to hear what he had to say. So he hired a consultant to run future meetings. The consultant didn't represent a hierarchical threat and was therefore able to get lots of participation from team members.

Another structural intervention might be to create smaller working groups of mixed cultures or mixed corporate identities in order to get at information that is not forthcoming from the team as a whole. The manager of the team that was evaluating retail opportunities in Japan used this approach. When she realized that the female Japanese consultants would not participate if the group got large, or if their male superior was present, she broke the team up into smaller groups to try to solve problems. She used this technique repeatedly and made a point of changing the subgroups' membership each time so that team members got to know and respect everyone else on the team.

The subgrouping technique involves risks, however. It buffers people who are not working well together or not participating in the larger group for one reason or another. Sooner or later the team will have to assemble the pieces that the subgroups have come up with, so this approach relies on another structural intervention: Someone must become a mediator in order to see that the various pieces fit together.

Managerial intervention

When a manager behaves like an arbitrator or a judge, making a final decision without team involvement, neither the manager nor the team gains much insight into why the team has stalemated. But it is possible for team members to use managerial intervention effectively to sort out problems.

When an American refinery-safety expert with significant experience throughout East Asia got stymied during a project in China, she called in her company's higher-level managers in Beijing to talk to the higher-level managers to whom the Chinese refinery's managers reported. Unlike the Western team members who breached etiquette by approaching the superiors of their Korean counterparts, the safety expert made sure to respect hierarchies in both organizations.

"Trying to resolve the issues," she told us, "the local management at the Chinese refinery would end up having conferences with our Beijing office and also with the upper management within the refinery. Eventually they understood that we weren't trying to insult them or their culture or to tell them they were bad in any way. We were trying to help. They eventually understood that there were significant fire and safety issues. But we actually had to go up some levels of management to get those resolved."

Managerial intervention to set norms early in a team's life can really help the team start out with effective processes. In one instance reported to us, a multicultural software development team's lingua franca was English, but some members, though they spoke grammatically correct English, had a very pronounced accent. In setting the ground rules for the team, the manager addressed the challenge directly, telling the members that they had been chosen for their task expertise, not their fluency in English, and that the team was going to have to work around language problems. As the project moved to the customer-services training stage, the manager advised the team members to acknowledge their accents up front. She said they should tell customers, "I realize I have an accent. If you don't understand what I'm saying, just stop me and ask questions."

Exit

Possibly because many of the teams we studied were project based, we found that leaving the team was an infrequent strategy for managing challenges. In short-term situations, unhappy team members often just waited out the project. When teams were permanent, producing products or services, the exit of one or more members was a strategy of last resort, but it was used—either voluntarily or after a formal request from management. Exit was likely when emotions were running high and too much face had been lost on both sides to salvage the situation.

An American member of a multicultural consulting team described the conflict between two senior consultants, one a Greek woman and the other a Polish man, over how to approach problems: "The woman from Greece would say, 'Here's the way I think we should do it.' It would be something that she was in control of. The guy from Poland would say, 'I think we should actually do it this way instead.' The woman would kind of turn red in the face, upset, and say, 'I just don't think that's the right way of doing it.' It would definitely switch from just professional differences to personal differences.

"The woman from Greece ended up leaving the firm. That was a direct result of probably all the different issues going on between these people. It really just wasn't a good fit. I've found that oftentimes when you're in consulting, you have to adapt to the culture, obviously, but you have to adapt just as much to the style of whoever is leading the project."

Though multicultural teams face challenges that are not directly attributable to cultural differences, such differences underlay whatever problem needed to be addressed in many of the teams we studied. Furthermore, while serious in their own right when they have a negative effect on team functioning, cultural challenges may also unmask fundamental managerial problems. Managers who intervene early and set norms; teams and managers who structure social interaction and work to engage everyone on the team; and teams that can see problems as stemming from culture, not personality, approach challenges with good humor and creativity. Managers who have to intervene when the team has reached a stalemate may be able to get the team moving again, but they seldom empower it to help itself the next time a stalemate occurs.

When frustrated team members take some time to think through challenges and possible solutions themselves, it can make a huge difference. Take, for example, this story about a financial-services call center. The members of the call-center team were all fluent Spanish-speakers, but some were North Americans and some were Latin Americans. Team performance, measured by calls answered per hour, was lagging. One Latin American was taking twice as long with her calls as the rest of the team. She was handling callers' questions appropriately, but she was also engaging in chitchat. When her teammates confronted her for being a free rider (they resented having to make up for her low call rate), she immediately acknowledged the problem, admitting that she did not know how to end the call politely—chitchat being normal in her culture. They rallied to help her: Using their technology, they would break into any of her calls that went overtime, excusing themeselves to the customer, offering to take over the call, and saying that this employee was urgently needed to help out on a different call. The team's solution worked in the short run, and the employee got better at ending her calls in the long run.

In another case, the Indian manager of a multicultural team coordinating a companywide IT project found himself frustrated when he and a teammate from Singapore met with two Japanese members of the coordinating team to try to get the Japan section to deliver its part of the project. The Japanese members seemed to be saying yes, but in the Indian manager's view, their follow-through was insufficient. He considered and rejected the idea of going up the hierarchy to the Japanese team members' boss, and decided instead to try to build consensus with the whole Japanese IT team, not just the two members on the coordinating team. He and his Singapore teammate put together an eBusiness road show, took it to Japan, invited the whole IT team to view it at a lunch meeting, and walked through success stories about other parts of the organiza-tion that had aligned with the company's larger business priorities. It was rather subtle, he told us, but it worked. The Japanese IT team wanted to be spotlighted in future eBusiness road shows. In the end, the whole team worked well together—and no higher-level manager had to get involved.

Originally published in November 2006. Reprint R0611D

When Teams Can't Decide

by Bob Frisch

THE EXECUTIVE TEAM IS DELIBERATING about a critical strategic choice, but no matter how much time and effort the team members expend, they cannot reach a satisfactory decision. Then comes that uncomfortable moment when all eyes turn to the CEO. The team waits for the boss to make the final call, yet when it's made, few people like the decision. Blame, though unspoken, is plentiful. The CEO blames the executives for indecisiveness; they resent the CEO for acting like a dictator. If this sounds familiar, you've experienced what I call the *dictator-by-default syndrome*.

For decades this dynamic has been diagnosed as a problem of leadership or teamwork or both. To combat it, companies use team-building and communications exercises that teach executives how to have assertive conversations, give and receive feedback, and establish mutual trust. In doing so, they miss the real problem, which lies not with the people but with the process. This sort of impasse is inherent in the act of arriving at a collective preference on the basis of individual preferences. Once leadership teams understand that voting-system mathematics are the culprit, they can stop wasting time on irrelevant psychological exercises and instead adopt practical measures designed to break the impasse. These measures, proven effective in scores of strategy off-sites for companies of all sizes, enable teams to move beyond the blame cycle to a no-fault style of decision making.

Asking the Impossible

Reaching collective decisions based on individual preferences is an imperfect science. Majority wishes can clash when a group of three or more people attempts to set priorities among three or more items. This "voting paradox," first noted in the eighteenth century by the Marquis de Condorcet, a French mathematician and social theorist, arises because different subsets of the group can generate conflicting majorities for all possible alternatives (see the exhibit "The voting paradox"). A century and a half later, renowned economist Ken Arrow developed his impossibility theorem, which established a series of mathematical proofs based on Condorcet's work.

Suppose a nine-person leadership team that wants to cut costs is weighing three options: (a) closing plants, (b) moving from a direct sales force to distributors, and (c) reducing benefits and pay. While any individual executive may be able to "rack and stack" her preferences,

---

The voting paradox: The boss is always wrong

A management team is attempting to select a fleet vehicle for its company's senior executives. When asked to rank three choices—BMW, Lexus, and Mercedes—the individual team members reach an impasse.

To break it, the CEO intervenes and picks BMW. But as the table shows, two-thirds of the team would have preferred a Lexus. Had he chosen Lexus, however, two-thirds of the team would have preferred Mercedes. And had he chosen Mercedes, two-thirds of the team would have preferred BMW. Instead of being transitive—Lexus beats BMW; Mercedes beats Lexus; therefore Mercedes beats BMW—the choice is circular.

Whatever decision the boss makes, the majority of his team is rooting for a different option. Unjustly, but not surprisingly, he is considered a dictator.

	First choice	Second choice	Third choice
Lou	BMW	Mercedes	Lexus
Sue	Mercedes	Lexus	BMW
Stu	Lexus	BMW	Mercedes

Idea in Brief

When cross-functional teams have trouble making decisions, leaders blame psychological factors like mistrust or poor communication. But the problem isn't the team's people; it's the decision-making process. Each member has constituencies in the organization. So each vies for resources for favored projects—virtually guaranteeing an impasse. To break the impasse, the team leader makes a unilateral decision, leaving a majority of the team disgruntled and resentful of the "dictator."

To improve your team's decision-making process, Frisch recommends several tactics. For example, clearly articulate the outcome your team must achieve. When people understand the goal, they more readily agree on how to get there. And surface members' functional preferences through pre-meeting surveys to identify areas of agreement and disagreement and to gauge the potential for deadlock.

These deceptively simple tactics position your team to prevent stalemates—instead of forcing you to be "dictator-by-default."

it's possible for a majority to be simultaneously found for each alternative. Five members might prefer "closing plants" to "moving sales to distributors" ($a > b$), and a different set of five might prefer "moving sales" to "reducing benefits and pay" ($b > c$). By the transitive property, "closing plants" should be preferred to "reducing benefits and pay" ($a > c$). But the paradox is that five members could rank "reducing benefits and pay" over "closing plants" ($c > a$). Instead of being transitive, the preferences are circular.

When the CEO is finally forced to choose an option, only a minority of team members will agree with the decision. No matter which option is selected, it's likely that different majorities will prefer alternative outcomes. Moreover, as Arrow demonstrated, no voting method—not allocation of points to alternatives, not rank-ordering of choices, nothing—can solve the problem. It can be circumvented but not cured.

Although the concept is well understood in political science and economics and among some organizational theorists, it hasn't yet crossed over to practical management. Understanding this paradox could greatly alter the way executive teams make decisions.

Idea in Practice

Frisch suggests these tactics for improving your team's decision-making process.

Specify the Desired Outcome

Without clear desired outcomes, team members choose options based on unspoken, differing assumptions. This sets the stage for the dictator-by-default syndrome. To avoid the syndrome, articulate what you want the team to accomplish.

> *Example:* A division of an industrial company was running out of manufacturing capacity for a product made in the U.S. The leadership team assumed the desired outcome was "Achieve the highest possible return on assets." So they discussed shuttering a U.S. plant and building a plant in China, where costs were lower and raw materials closer. But the parent company's

desired outcome was "Minimize corporate overhead and maximize earnings." The move to China would mean closing an additional facility that supplied materials to the U.S. plant, significantly lowering earnings. Once the division team understood the desired outcome, it could solve the capacity problem in a way that was consistent with the parent's actual goals.

Provide a Range of Options for Achieving the Desired Outcome

Break alternatives into a broader range of options beyond "Accept the proposed plan," "Reject the plan," and "Defer the decision."

Test Fences and Walls

When team members cite a presumed boundary (for example, a real or imagined corporate policy), ask "Is it a wall (it's

Acknowledging the Problem

To circumvent the dictator-by-default syndrome, CEOs and their teams must first understand the conditions that give rise to it. The syndrome is perhaps most obvious at executive off-sites, but it can crop up in any executive committee meeting of substance.

Most executive teams are, in effect, legislatures. With the exception of the CEO, each member represents a significant constituency in the organization, from marketing to operations to finance. No matter how many times a CEO asks team members to take off their relatively immovable) or is it a fence (it can be moved)?"

Example: For a division of a global financial services provider, executives never considered expanding their offerings to include banking services. That's because they thought corporate policy prohibited entry into banking. When the division head tested this assumption with her boss, she learned that the real concern was not to do anything that would bring new regulatory requirements (the wall). So the division developed strategic options that included several features of banking that avoided dealing with new regulations.

Surface Preferences Early

Survey members before meetings to identify their preferences and focus the subsequent discussion.

Example: A global credit card company was deciding where to invest in growth. Executive team members conducted a straw poll of countries under consideration. The process enabled them to quickly eliminate countries that attracted no votes. And it focused their subsequent discussion on the two regions where there was most agreement.

Assign Devil's Advocates

Make thorough and dispassionate counterarguments an expected part of strategic deliberations. Assign devil's advocates to make the case against each option. This depersonalizes the discussion and produces more nuanced strategy discussions.

functional hats and view the organization holistically, the executives find it difficult to divorce themselves from their functional responsibilities. Because the team often focuses on assigning resources and setting priorities, members vie for allocations and approval for favored projects. When more than two options are on the table, the scene is set for the CEO to become a dictator by default.

More insidiously, the problem exists even when a team is considering an either/or choice, despite the fact that the voting paradox requires three or more options. Framing strategy considerations as binary choices—"We must either aggressively enter this market or get out of this line of business altogether"—appears to avert the problem. However, such choices always include a third, implied alternative: "Neither of the above." In other words, there could be circular majorities for entering the market, for exiting the business, and for doing neither.

Take, for example, the ubiquitous business case, which usually offers a single, affirmative recommendation: "We should aggressively enter this market now." The only apparent alternative is to forgo the market—but some team members may want to enter it more tentatively, others may want to enter an adjacent market, and still others may want to defer the decision until the market potential becomes clearer.

The use of the business case, which forces decisions into a yes-or-no framework, is a tacit admission that groups are not good at discussing and prioritizing multiple options. Further, when a team of analysts has spent six months working up the business case and only a half hour has been allotted to the item on the agenda, dissenting team members may be reluctant to speak up. Questions from the heads of sales and marketing, who have spent only a day or two with a briefing book and 20 minutes watching a PowerPoint presentation, would most likely be treated as comments tossed from the peanut gallery. So the team remains silent and unwittingly locked in the voting paradox. Ultimately, in order to move on to the next agenda item, either the team appears to reach a majority view or the CEO issues a fiat. In reality, however, there may be competing opinions, alternative majority opinions, and dissatisfaction with the outcome—all of them unstated.

Managing the Impossible

Once CEOs and their teams understand why they have trouble making decisions, they can adopt some straightforward tactics to minimize potential dysfunction.

Articulate clearly what outcome you are seeking

It's surprising how often executives assume that they are talking about the same thing when in fact they are talking past one another. In a discussion of growth, for instance, some may be referring to revenue, others to market share, and others to net income. The discussion should begin with agreement on what outcome the team is trying to achieve. If it's growth, then do all the members agree on which measures are most relevant?

In the absence of clearly articulated goals, participants will choose options based on unspoken, often widely differing, premises, creating a situation that is ripe for the dictator-by-default syndrome. One division of a major industrial company, for example, was running out of manufacturing capacity for a commodity product made in the United States and a specialty product made in Western Europe. Because costs of labor and raw materials were high in both places, the leadership team was considering what seemed like an obvious choice: shutting down the U.S. plant and building a plant in China, where costs were lower and raw materials were closer, to handle the commodity business and any growth in the specialty business. Most members of the team assumed that the desired outcome was to achieve the highest possible return on net assets, which the move to China might well have accomplished.

However, the CEO had been in discussions with corporate managers who were primarily concerned with allocation of overhead throughout the enterprise. The move to China would mean shutting down an additional plant that supplied raw materials to the U.S. plant, with implications for corporate earnings. Once the division team fully understood what outcome the parent company desired—to minimize overhead costs without taking a hit on earnings—it could work on solving the capacity problem in a way that honored the parent's strictures.

It's essential to keep discussion of the desired outcome distinct from discussion about how to achieve it. Sometimes, simply articulating the desired outcome will forestall or dissolve disagreement about solutions because the options can be tested against an accepted premise. It may also help avert the political horse trading that can occur when executives try to protect their interests rather than aiming for a common goal.

Provide a range of options for achieving outcomes

Once the team at the industrial company had articulated the desired outcome, it could break the simplistic "accept," "reject," and "defer" alternatives into a more nuanced range of options: build a specialty plant in China; beef up the plant in Western Europe; or build a commodity plant in China and gradually decommission the U.S. plant.

Test fences and walls

When teams are invited to think about options, they almost immediately focus on what they *can't* do—especially at the divisional level, where they may feel hemmed in by corporate policies, real or imagined. Often the entire team not only assumes that a constraint is real but also shies away when the discussion comes anywhere near it. When team members cite a presumed boundary, my colleagues and I encourage them to ask whether it's a wall, which can't be moved, or a fence, which can.

For example, one division of a global provider of financial services was looking at new avenues for growth. Although expanding the division's offerings to include banking services was a promising possibility, the executive team never considered it, assuming that corporate policy prohibited the company from entering banking. When the division head explicitly tested that assumption with her boss, she found that the real prohibition—the wall—was against doing anything that would bring certain types of new regulatory requirements. With that knowledge, the division's executive team was able to develop strategic options that included some features of banking but avoided any new regulations.

Surface preferences early

Like juries, executive teams can get an initial sense of where they stand by taking nonbinding votes early in the discussion. They can also conduct surveys in advance of meetings in order to identify areas of agreement and disagreement as well as the potential for deadlock.

A global credit card company was deciding where to invest in growth. Ordinarily, executive team members would have embarked on an open-ended discussion in which numerous countries would be under consideration; that tactic would have invited the possibility of multiple majorities. Instead, they conducted a straw poll, quickly eliminating the countries that attracted no votes and focusing their subsequent discussion on the two places where there was the most agreement.

Using weighted preferences is another way to narrow the decision-making field and help prevent the dictator-by-default syndrome. The life and annuities division of a major insurance company had developed a business plan that included a growth in profit of $360 million. The executive team was trying to determine which line of business would deliver that growth. Instead of casting equally weighted votes for various lines of business, each executive was given poker chips representing $360 million and a grid with squares representing the company's products and channels. Team members distributed their chips according to where they thought the projected growth was likely to be found. After discussing the results they repeated the exercise, finding that some agreement emerged.

By the third and final round of the exercise, this weighted voting had helped them narrow their discussion to a handful of businesses and channels, and genuine alignment began to develop among team members. Equally weighted votes might have locked the executive team into the voting paradox, but this technique dissolved the false equality of alternatives that is often at the root of the problem. Proposing options early and allowing people to tailor them reduces the likelihood that executives will be forced into a stalemate that the CEO has to break.

State each option's pros and cons

Rather than engaging in exercises about giving feedback or learning how to have assertive conversations, executives can better spend their time making sure that both sides of every option are forcefully voiced. That may require a devil's advocate.

The concept of a devil's advocate originated in the Roman Catholic Church's canonization process, in which a lawyer is appointed to argue against the canonization of a candidate—even the most apparently saintly. Similarly, in law, each side files its own brief; the defense doesn't simply respond off-the-cuff to the plaintiff's argument.

In business, however, an advocate for a particular option typically delivers a presentation that may contain some discussion of risk but remains entirely the work of someone who is sold on the idea. Members of the executive team are expected to agree with the business case or attack it, although they may have seen it only a few days before the meeting and thus have no way of producing an equally detailed rebuttal or offering solid alternatives. Further, attacking the business case is often perceived as attacking the person who is presenting it. Frequently the only executives with open license to ask tough, probing questions are the CEO and the CFO, but even they lack the detailed knowledge of the team advocating the business case.

By breaking the false binary of a business case into several explicit and implicit alternatives and assigning a devil's advocate to critique each option, you can depersonalize the discussion, making thorough and dispassionate counterarguments an expected part of strategic deliberations. This approach is especially valuable when the preferences of the CEO or other powerful members of the team are well known. If assigning a devil's advocate to each option appears too cumbersome, try a simpler variant: Have the CEO or a meeting facilitator urge each team member to offer two or three suggestions from the perspective of his functional area. Instead of unreasonably asking executives to think like a CEO, which usually elicits silence or perfunctory comments, this tactic puts team members on the solid ground of their expertise and transforms an unsatisfying false binary into far more options for discussion.

A major internet entertainment company adopted a novel version of the devil's advocate approach. The company maintains a council to consider its many potential investments, from upgrading its server farms to adopting new technology to creating special entertainment events on the web. In the past, each opportunity was presented to the council as a business case by an advocate of the investment, and each case was evaluated in isolation.

Frustrated with this haphazard approach, the company established a new system: The council now considers all investment proposals as a portfolio at its monthly strategy meetings. All proposals follow an identical template, allowing for easy comparison and a uniform scoring system. Finally, each one needs sign-off from an independent executive.

This system incorporates the devil's advocate role at two levels. For each proposal the validating executive, not wishing to be accountable for groundless optimism, considers carefully all of the counterarguments, does a reality check, and makes sure the sponsor adjusts the score accordingly. At the portfolio level, the comparative-scoring system reminds the team that the proposals are competing for limited resources, which prompts a more critical assessment.

Devise new options that preserve the best features of existing ones

Despite a team's best efforts, executives can still find themselves at an impasse. That is a measure of both the weightiness of some strategic decisions and the intractability of the voting paradox—it's not necessarily an index of executive dysfunction.

Teams should continue to reframe their options in ways that preserve their original intent, be it a higher return on net assets or greater growth. When they feel the impulse to shoehorn decisions into an either/or framework, they should step back and generate a broader range of options. For instance, the executive team of the property and casualty division of a large insurer wanted to grow either by significantly increasing the company's share with existing agencies or by increasing the total number of agencies that sold its products. Before the leadership team took either path, it needed to decide whether to offer a full line of products or a narrow line. As a result, team members found themselves considering four business models: (1) full product line, existing large agencies; (2) narrow product line, existing large agencies; (3) full product line, more small agencies; and (4) narrow product line, more small agencies. Dissatisfied with those choices, they broke the business down into 16 value attributes, including brand, claim service, agency compensation, price competitiveness, breadth of product offering, and agency-facing technology. Some of these value attributes might apply to all four of the original business models; others to three or fewer. Agent-facing technology, for example, is typical of working with many small agencies, because their sheer numbers preclude high-touch relationships with each one.

The team then graded its company and several competitors on each attribute to find competitive openings that fit with the division's willingness and ability to invest. Instead of four static choices, it now had a much larger number of choices based on different combinations of value attributes. Ultimately, it chose to bring several lagging attributes up to market standard, elevate others to above-market standard, and aggressively emphasize still others. This turned out to be a far less radical redirection than the team had originally assumed was needed.

Two Essential Ground Rules

So far, I have outlined several tactics that leadership teams can use to circumvent the dictator-by-default syndrome. These tactics can be effective whether they are used singly or in tandem. But if teams are to thwart this syndrome, they must adhere to two ground rules.

Deliberate confidentially

A secure climate for the conversation is essential to allow team members to float trial balloons and cut deals. An executive who knows that her speculative remarks about closing plants may be circulated throughout the company will be reluctant to engage in the free play of mind that unfettered strategy discussion demands. Moreover, team members whose priorities don't prevail in the deliberations must be able to save face when the meeting is over. If they are known to have "lost" or to have relinquished something dear to their constituents, their future effectiveness as leaders might be undermined.

Deliberate over an appropriate time frame
All too often the agendas for strategy off-sites contain items like "China market strategy," with 45 minutes allotted for the decision. The result is a discussion that goes nowhere or an arbitrary decision by the CEO that runs roughshod over competing majorities for other options. When new options are devised or existing ones unbundled, team members need time to study them carefully and assess the counterarguments. Breaking up the discussion into several meetings spaced widely apart and interspersed with additional analysis and research gives people a chance to reconsider their preferences. It also gives them time to prepare their constituencies for changes that are likely to emerge as a result of a new strategy.

———————————

Leadership and communication exercises have their merits. A team can't make effective decisions if its members don't trust one another or if they fail to listen to one another. The problem I see most often, however, is one that simply cannot be fixed with the psychological tools so often touted in management literature. If executives employ the tactics described here, which are designed to fix the decision-making process, they will have far greater success in achieving real alignment.

Originally published in November 2008. Reprint R0811J

Virtuoso Teams

by Bill Fischer and Andy Boynton

BLOOD ON THE STAGE, RACIAL tensions turned violent, dissonant music, and dancing hoodlums—*West Side Story* was anything but the treacly Broadway musical typical of the late 1950s. It was a high-stakes, radical innovation that fundamentally changed the face of American popular drama. The movie version earned ten Oscars. Not a bad achievement for the team of virtuosos—choreographer Jerome Robbins, writer Arthur Laurents, composer Leonard Bernstein, and lyricist Stephen Sondheim—who created it.

In nearly any area of human achievement—business, the arts, science, athletics, politics—you can find teams that produce outstanding and innovative results. The business world offers a few examples. Think of the Whiz Kids—the team of ten former U.S. Air Force officers recruited en masse in 1946—who brought Ford back from the doldrums. Recall Seymour Cray and his team of "supermen" who, in the early 1960s, developed the very first commercially available supercomputer, far outpacing IBM's most powerful processor. More recently, consider Microsoft's Xbox team, which pulled off the unthinkable by designing a gaming platform that put serious pressure on the top-selling Sony PlayStation 2 in its first few months on the market.

We call such work groups *virtuoso teams,* and they are fundamentally different from the garden-variety groups that most organizations form to pursue more modest goals. Virtuoso teams comprise the elite experts in their particular fields and are specially convened for ambitious projects. Their work style has a frenetic rhythm. They emanate a discernible energy. They are utterly unique in the ambitiousness of their goals, the intensity of their conversations, the degree of their esprit, and the extraordinary results they deliver.

Despite such potential, most companies deliberately avoid virtuoso teams, thinking that the risks are too high. For one thing, it's tough to keep virtuoso teams together once they achieve their goals—burnout and the lure of new challenges rapidly winnow the ranks. For another, most firms consider expert individuals to be too elitist, temperamental, egocentric, and difficult to work with. Force such people to collaborate on a high-stakes project and they just might come to fisticuffs. Even the very notion of managing such a group seems unimaginable. So most organizations fall into default mode, setting up project teams of people who get along nicely. The result is mediocrity. We've seen the pattern often.

For the past six years, we've studied the inner workings of teams charged with important projects in 20 of the world's best-known companies. We've found that some teams with big ambitions and considerable talent systematically fail, sometimes before our very eyes. In interviewing the managers involved, we discovered that virtuoso teams play by a different set of rules than other teams. The several dozen high-performance teams we studied, drawn from diverse fields, fit a few overarching criteria. Not only did they accomplish their enormous goals, but they also changed their businesses, their customers, even their industries.

Unlike traditional teams—which are typically made up of whoever's available, regardless of talent—virtuoso teams consist of star performers who are handpicked to play specific, key roles. These teams are intense and intimate, and they work best when members are forced together in cramped spaces under strict time constraints. They assume that their customers are every bit as smart and sophisticated as they are, so they don't cater to a stereotypical "average." Leaders of virtuoso teams put a premium on great collaboration—and they're not afraid to encourage creative confrontation to get it.

Among the work groups we studied were two from outside the mainstream business world—the creative teams behind *West Side*

Idea in Brief

Imagine these high-stakes scenarios: Your company must enter an untested new market. Or reorganize to take advantage of a new IT platform. Or avert a public relations crisis brought on by product tampering. To manage such feats, you need **virtuoso teams**—groups of top experts in their fields.

But superstars are notorious for being temperamental and egocentric. You worry that forcing a group of them to work together will ignite a fatal explosion. So you're tempted to settle for an ordinary project team instead.

Don't do it. Ordinary teams may play nice, but they produce results as unremarkable as themselves. Assemble your virtuoso team—and manage it with counterintuitive strategies, advise Fischer and Boynton.

For example, instead of emphasizing the collective, celebrate individual egos by creating opportunities for solo performances. Then build *group* ego by encouraging a single-minded focus on the goal. And foster impassioned, direct dialogue that doesn't spare feelings. In the resulting inferno, your team's members will forge their most brilliant ideas.

Story and the 1950s-era television hit *Your Show of Shows* and its successors. Both teams were vivid, unique, and, ultimately, managed to change their very competitive businesses. We also offer a more current business example from Norsk Hydro, the Norwegian energy giant. We intently studied a variety of sources, including diaries, interviews, video archive materials, and the impressions of many of the principals involved. In the following pages, we'll describe in more detail what constitutes a virtuoso team, how these teams work, and what they require in the way of leadership.

Assemble the Stars

Most traditional teams are more concerned with doing than with thinking. In other words, the working assumption is that execution is more important than generating breakthrough ideas. Team assignments, therefore, fall to people who seem to be able to get the work done. A less conventional approach, however, is more likely to produce exceptional results.

Idea in Practice

Fischer and Boynton suggest these principles for leading a virtuoso team.

Assemble the stars. Hire only members with the best skills, even if they have little experience with the problem at hand.

> *Example:* After investing heavily in a site promising a big oil find, Norsk Hydro discovered the site was dry. Team leader Kjell Sunde assembled a virtuoso team to avert an investor-relations crisis. The team included the best technical people from across the company. Its goal: Analyze reams of data, pinpoint what went wrong, and convince stakeholders such an outcome wouldn't occur again.

Build the group ego. As your team's project progresses, help stars break through their egocentrism and morph into a powerful, unified team with a shared identity.

> *Example:* Sunde initially broke with Norsk Hydro's consensus-driven culture by publicly celebrating his team members and putting them squarely in the spotlight. He established a star mentality by nicknaming them the "A-team." Then he built the team's group ego by protecting members from intrusive scrutiny from above, giving them unlimited access to resources, and treating their conclusions as definitive.

Make work a contact sport. Use face-to-face conversations in designated spaces to foster impassioned dialogue.

> *Example:* Sunde established a dedicated team room and filled

In virtuoso teams, thinking is more important than doing: Individual members are hired for their skills and their willingness to dive into big challenges. Instead of assembling a variety of individuals and averaging their talents down to a mean, virtuoso team leaders push each player hard to reach his or her potential within the overall context of the team objective. Virtuoso team members are not shy; they typically want to take on a risky venture that can pull them away from their well-trodden paths. They love daunting challenges, and they accept the risk of exposure and career damage if their projects fail. The risk increases pressure on the team to deliver; accordingly, the individual members give their utmost to assure that radical innovation happens.

it with computer workstations and other scientific and communications equipment. The space functioned as a workroom and meeting place for candid, intense discussions that let members bounce ideas off each other.

Respect the customer's intelligence. Foster the belief that your team's customers want more, not less. You'll encourage them to deliver solutions consistent with this higher perception.

> *Example:* For Norsk Hydro's A-team, "customers" were equity market analysts. The team's job was to manage the market's reaction to news of the dry site. If its explanation was slapdash or incomplete, the company's market value would nosedive. The team provided thoughtful explanations that left

market analysts impressed with the firm's ability to respond convincingly and quickly to market concerns. The company received kudos in the press and was spared serious financial erosion.

Herd the cats. Use time management strategies to balance team members' need for individual attention and intellectual freedom with the uncompromising demands and time lines of your high-stakes project.

> *Example:* Sunde forced A-team members to keep presentations to 15 minutes. That encouraged members to use this allotment to maximum effect and discouraged aggressive members from imposing their viewpoints on others. The strong adherence to time "made everyone aware they had to dance to the same rhythm."

If you want great performances of any type, you have to start with great people. In 1949, a young comic named Sid Caesar distanced himself from his competition by relying on a group of virtuoso writers including Neil Simon, Mel Brooks, Carl Reiner, and Woody Allen. *Your Show of Shows* and Caesar's other weekly productions were the biggest commercial successes on TV at the time. Week after week over a period of nine years, Caesar and his cadre of writers created live, consistently award-winning performances in a string of TV comedy hits. Mel Brooks famously likened the group to a World Series ball club, echoing the sentiments of many who acclaimed the team as the greatest writing staff in the history of television.

They may have been the best comedy writers in America—but they weren't the nicest. As is the case with all virtuoso teams, Caesar's staffers engaged daily in high-energy contests. It was as if each writer knew he or she was the best; every day, each tried to top the others for the "best of the best" title. The interpersonal conflict often intensified as the writers jostled aggressively to see whose ideas would be accepted. Mel Brooks frequently irritated Max Liebman, producer of the *Admiral Broadway Revue* and *Your Show of Shows,* and vice versa: Liebman found Brooks arrogant and obnoxious, while Brooks, for his part, declared that he owed no allegiance to Liebman. The tension among team members led Caesar to describe the competitive atmosphere as one filled with "electricity and hate"; two other virtuosos translated Caesar's description into terms of "competition" and "collaboration."

The *West Side Story* group was also famously discordant. To build the team, Jerome Robbins, a young classical ballet choreographer with an impressive résumé, sought out Leonard Bernstein, one of the moving forces in classical music composition and conducting; Arthur Laurents, a highly regarded and successful screenwriter; and budding lyricist Stephen Sondheim. All of these talented players had enormous egos and greedy ambition. In their very first meeting, Laurents refused to play a subordinate role to the famously egotistical Bernstein, insisting vociferously that he was not about to write a libretto for any "goddamned Bernstein opera." All the team members engaged in similarly nasty tugs-of-war with one another. They needed each others' skills, not peace and quiet.

Build the Group Ego

Traditional teams typically operate under the tyranny of the "we"—that is, they put group consensus and constraint above individual freedom. Team harmony is important; conviviality compensates for missing talent. This produces teams with great attitudes and happy members, but, to paraphrase Liebman, "from a polite team comes a polite result."

Traditional teams versus virtuoso teams

Virtuoso teams differ from traditional teams along every dimension, from the way they recruit members to the way they enforce their processes and from the expectations they hold to the results they produce.

Traditional teams	Virtuoso teams
Choose members for availability	**Choose members for skills**
• Assign members according to the individuals' availability and past experience with the problem.	• Insist on hiring only those with the best skills, regardless of the individuals' familiarity with the problem.
• Fill in the team as needed.	• Recruit specialists for each position on the team.
Emphasize the collective	**Emphasize the individual**
• Repress individual egos.	• Celebrate individual egos and elicit the best from each team member.
• Encourage members to get along.	• Encourage members to compete, and create opportunities for solo performances.
• Choose a solution based on consensus.	• Choose a solution based on merit.
• Assure that efficiency trumps creativity.	• Assure that creativity trumps efficiency.
Focus on tasks	**Focus on ideas**
• Complete critical tasks on time.	• Generate a frequent and rich flow of ideas among team members.
• Get the project done on time.	• Find and express the breakthrough idea on time.
Work individually and remotely	**Work together and intensively**
• Require individual members to complete tasks on their own.	• Force members into close physical proximity.
• Allow communication via e-mail, phone, and weekly meetings.	• Force members to work together at a fast pace.
• Encourage polite conversations.	• Force direct dialogue without sparing feelings.
Address the average customer	**Address the sophisticated customer**
• Attempt to reach the broadest possible customer base; appeal to the average.	• Attempt to surprise customers by stretching their expectations; appeal to the sophisticate.
• Base decisions on established market knowledge.	• Defy established market knowledge.
• Affirm common stereotypes.	• Reject common stereotypes.

When virtuoso teams begin their work, individuals are in and group consensus is out. As the project progresses, however, the individual stars harness themselves to the product of the group. Sooner or later, the members break through their own egocentrism and become a plurality with a single-minded focus on the goal. In short, they morph into a powerful team with a shared identity.

Consider how Norsk Hydro used a virtuoso team to handle a looming investor relations crisis. In 2002, Bloc 34, the potential site for a big oil find in Angola, turned out to be dry. Hydro had made a serious investment in the site. Somehow, senior management would have to convincingly explain the company's failure to the financial markets or Hydro's stock could plummet.

The senior managers understood that this problem was too critical to leave to conventional approaches, but Hydro was certainly not a natural environment for a virtuoso team. Rich in heritage, unwieldy, and traditional, with a strong engineering culture and a decidedly Nordic consensus-driven approach to decisions, the company never singled out or recognized individual performers. In fact, most of Hydro's business activities were specialized and separated. Teamwork was satisfactory but unexceptional, and tension among employees was firmly discouraged.

Defying precedent, team leader Kjell Sunde assembled a high-powered group comprising the very best technical people from across the company. Their task? To review a massive stream of data—one that had occupied the minds of some of the best professionals for more than four years. Their goal? To understand what had gone wrong in the original analysis of Bloc 34 and to assure key stakeholders that the company would prevent such an outcome from occurring again. Their deadline? A completely unreasonable six weeks.

Sunde's challenge was to strike a delicate balance between stroking the egos of the elites and focusing them on the task at hand. Each of the brilliant technologists was supremely confident in his abilities. Each had a reputation for being egocentric and difficult. Each had a tendency to dominate and aggressively seek the limelight. In a consensus-driven company like Hydro, the typical modus operandi would have been to exhort the individuals to surrender their egos and play nicely together.

But Sunde went in the opposite direction, completely breaking with corporate culture by publicly celebrating the selected members and putting them squarely in the spotlight. The Bloc 34 Task Force, nicknamed the "A-team," established a star mentality from its very inception. Selection for the project was clearly a sign of trust in each member's ability to perform outstanding work on a seemingly impossible task. For the most part, the members knew one another already, which eliminated the need for them to build polite relationships and helped them jump in right away.

Sunde then set about building the A-team's group ego. He guaranteed the members the respect they craved by assuring them that they would work autonomously—there would be no micromanagement or intrusive scrutiny from above. Team members would have absolute top priority and access to any resources they required, their conclusions would be definitive, and there would be no second-guessing. All this set a positive tone and bolstered group morale.

Still, there were plenty of early clashes. To control the friction, Sunde introduced an overall pattern to the teamwork. First, he paired off individual team members in accordance with their expertise and his sense of their psychological fit. Each half of the couple worked on a separate but related problem, and each pair's problem set fit together with the other sets to form the overall puzzle, which team members had to keep in mind as they worked.

Eventually, each team member understood that if the team failed, he would fail too. This kept any of the members from developing an entrenched sense of idea ownership. As it worked, the team transformed itself from a collection of egocentric individuals into one great totality. Had the group started out as a cohesive whole, individual talents might never have been realized and harnessed to the goal.

Make Work a Contact Sport

Typical teams are all too often spatially dispersed—they are managed remotely and get together only occasionally for debate and discussion. Most of the time, such a scenario works quite well. But when big change and high performance are required, these standard working conditions fall short of the mark. In virtuoso teams, individual players energize each other and stimulate ideas with frequent, intense, face-to-face conversations, often held in cramped spaces over long periods of time. The usual rounds of e-mails, phone calls, and occasional meetings just don't cut it.

When virtuoso teams are in action, impassioned dialogue becomes the critical driver of performance, not the work itself. The inescapable physical proximity of team members ensures that the right messages get to the right people—fast. As a result, virtuoso teams operate at a pace that is many times the speed of normal project teams.

Your Show of Shows and Caesar's other TV programs were developed each week in a small, chaotic suite of rooms on the sixth floor of 130 West 56th Street in Manhattan. Experimentation and rapid prototyping were the name of the game; only the best ideas survived. One team member compared the daily atmosphere to a Marx Brothers movie: People shouted at the top of their lungs; piles of food and cigarette butts lay everywhere. The pace was dizzying, yet everyone stayed focused. The pressure-cooker environment resulted in fierce interpersonal clashes, but there wasn't time to sulk or stay angry. The tight work space and relentless deadlines created a cauldron of energy and a frenzy of ideas.

Members of Norsk Hydro's A-team joked that they were not a task force; rather, they were "forced to task." Sunde established a dedicated room for the team and filled it with computer workstations and other necessary scientific and communications equipment. The space functioned both as a workroom and as a common meeting place (members of the team spent as much as 90 hours per week together). The atmosphere was relaxed and informal, and the discussions that took place there were open, honest, and passionate. Team members "would continually interact," Sunde said, "bouncing ideas off each other and to a degree competing, or at least keeping their eyes on each other."

The intense pressure on virtuoso teams affects project duration as well. These work groups usually break up for one of two reasons: Either the sheer physical, intellectual, and emotional demands take their toll (though *Your Show of Shows* and the team's other comedy hits lasted for nine years, there was high turnover within the writing group) or the stars, who are always in high demand, find themselves drawn to other new and challenging projects. Still, as long as the team members remain passionately interested and feel they have the opportunity to leave a significant mark on their company or their industry, they will work long and hard.

Challenge the Customer

Virtuoso teams believe that customers want more, not less, and that they can appreciate the richness of an aggrandized proposition. Virtuoso teams deliver solutions that are consistent with this higher perception. The vision of the demanding customer becomes a self-fulfilling prophecy, for while competitors create diminished offerings for their clients, virtuoso teams redefine taste and expectations and raise the level of market acceptability.

Before *West Side Story,* Broadway musicals were typically limited to a conventional formula of nostalgia, comedy, and feel-good endings. They were easily marketable entertainment. A typical hit of the day was *Damn Yankees,* a musical about a baseball fan who makes a pact with the devil. There was no room for tragedy, social critique, or even art on the Great White Way.

Robbins, Bernstein, Laurents, and Sondheim believed otherwise, but few agreed with them. Getting *West Side Story* to the stage was a huge challenge because most producers thought the project too risky, dealing as it did with themes of social consciousness and racial violence. How could it possibly make money? As venture capital dried up, Robbins and the others persisted, laying their careers on the line to bring audiences something totally new, daring, and different from anything they had experienced before. The enormous success of their project vindicated them.

Sid Caesar similarly believed that nothing was too much for his audience. At a time when American TV was beginning its long slide into programming mediocrity, Caesar wanted to get away from the crude, pie-in-the-face, seltzer-bottle slapstick that he found degrading. In a turnabout from convention, he and his team regularly presented audiences with challenging material. Liebman put it this way: "We take for granted . . . that the mass audience we're trying to reach isn't a dumb one. It has a high quota of intelligence, and there's no need to play down to it. . . . We strive for adult entertainment, without compromise, and believe that the audience will understand it."

For Norsk Hydro, the "customers" were the equity market analysts. The team members' job was to manage the market's reaction; if their explanation was slapdash or incomplete, the company's market value would nosedive. Faced with a similar situation, most businesses would have tried to downplay the fact that a gigantic project had failed, offering a pallid apology and then weathering the ensuing storm. Some companies, however, are able to turn these incidents to their advantage. (In 1988, for instance, an Ashland Oil storage tank ruptured while being filled. Diesel fuel damaged ecosystems and contaminated drinking water. The company's full disclosure and aggressive cleanup efforts restored its good name.) Likewise, Norsk Hydro turned the Bloc 34 incident to its advantage. The thoughtful explanations the virtuoso team provided left market analysts impressed with the firm's ability to respond convincingly and quickly to market concerns. The company received kudos in the press and was spared from any serious financial erosion.

Herd the Cats

Most leaders of traditional teams—even those working on big projects—emphasize consensus and compromise. Their goal is to keep stress levels low, meet deadlines, and produce acceptable results. By contrast, leaders of virtuoso teams must be far more deft and forceful. Their goal is to help individual performers, and the group as a whole, achieve their utmost potential.

The worst thing you can do to highly talented, independent people is to constrain their expressiveness; you have to trust and encourage their talents. At the same time, however, a team made up of these individuals must meet strict goals and deadlines. Balancing the virtuosos' needs for individual attention and intellectual freedom with the uncompromising demands and time lines of a high-stakes project requires unusual skill. For this reason, leaders of virtuoso teams assume different kinds of roles, and use different management tools, than do leaders of traditional teams.

One way to manage a virtuoso team is to be a rigid—even villainous—perfectionist. Jerome Robbins was a perfect example of this. He combined the unforgiving discipline of a boot camp sergeant with an artist's attention to detail. He pushed, prodded, embarrassed, and demanded excellence from his people; he overlooked no detail in an effort to capture the cast's total attention. For example, he posted articles about interracial gang warfare on the theater walls and encouraged others to find and share similar reports. Each gang-member character had a biography—for the first time on Broadway, there was to be no anonymous chorus—and actors were forbidden to use any other names in the theater. Robbins segregated the cast into their respective gangs. "This stage is the only piece of territory you really own in this theater," he barked. "Nothing else belongs to you. You've got to fight for it." This sparked genuine antagonism between the groups, which imbued the final production with verisimilitude.

Needless to say, tensions ran high, and the stress on individual players was enormous. In the end, many cast members hated Robbins (one thespian observed, "If I go to Hell, I will not be afraid of the devil. Because I have worked with Jerome Robbins."). Still, his hard-nosed leadership won him great respect. Chita Rivera, who starred as Anita in the Broadway version of *West Side Story,* noted that "...if [Robbins] hadn't been the way he was, none of those people would have danced the way they did. None of them would have had the careers that they had...because people give up, we all give up, and we give up a lot of times too soon. He made you do what you were really capable of doing, something you never even dreamed you could possibly do."

Other leaders of virtuoso teams take the opposite tack: They strive for excellence by fostering a galloping sense of intellectual and creative freedom in individuals and in the group as a whole. Sid Caesar let his team members express themselves as freely as possible and encouraged creative pandemonium. Though the process might have looked chaotic to an outside observer—and to NBC's management—Caesar kept the group focused on the goal: to produce the very best comedy possible for each show. His team members would work shoulder to shoulder to write and rewrite the same scene many times in the same week—sometimes in the same day—in a frantic effort to perfect it through repeated testing. Ideas, situations, and lines would be tossed back and forth, and, though most would be rejected, a choice few would be accepted and pursued. In the brainstorming maelstrom, ownership of the ideas was difficult to pinpoint. This created a sense of mutual respect and unity in the group; the writers felt they belonged to something bigger than themselves. "He had total control, but we had total freedom," writer Larry Gelbart, a contributor to *Your Show of Shows,* said of Caesar's management style. This statement goes to the very heart of what it means to lead a virtuoso team.

Regardless of their personal approaches, all leaders of virtuoso teams exploit time as a management tool. At Norsk Hydro, Sunde used time in a very specific way. Because presentations were kept to a strict limit of 15 minutes, members used their allotment to maximum effect. And the time limit prevented the more aggressive members from imposing their points of view on others. The deadline pressure was so great that the team had no choice but to maintain its focus on the task at hand. As one technologist put it, the strong adherence to time "made everyone aware that they had to dance to the same rhythm."

Companies in every industry pursue ambitious projects all the time, tackling big product changes, new market entries, and large reorganizations. But when breakthrough performance is called for, it's clear that business as usual won't suffice.

If you want to stamp out mediocrity, remember the instructive lessons from Sid Caesar's writers' group, the *West Side Story* team, and Norsk Hydro's A-team: Don't hesitate to assemble the very best and let their egos soar. Encourage intense dialogue—and then watch as the sparks fly. If you allow the most brilliant minds in your organization to collide and create, the result will be true excellence.

Originally published in July 2005. Reprint R0507K

How Management Teams Can Have a Good Fight

by Kathleen M. Eisenhardt, Jean L. Kahwajy, and L.J. Bourgeois III

TOP MANAGERS ARE OFTEN STYMIED by the difficulties of managing conflict. They know that conflict over issues is natural and even necessary. Reasonable people, making decisions under conditions of uncertainty, are likely to have honest disagreements over the best path for their company's future. Management teams whose members challenge one another's thinking develop a more complete understanding of the choices, create a richer range of options, and ultimately make the kinds of effective decisions necessary in today's competitive environments.

But, unfortunately, healthy conflict can quickly turn unproductive. A comment meant as a substantive remark can be interpreted as a personal attack. Anxiety and frustration over difficult choices can evolve into anger directed at colleagues. Personalities frequently become intertwined with issues. Because most executives pride themselves on being rational decision makers, they find it difficult even to acknowledge—let alone manage—this emotional, irrational dimension of their behavior.

The challenge—familiar to anyone who has ever been part of a management team—is to keep constructive conflict over issues from degenerating into dysfunctional interpersonal conflict, to encourage managers to argue without destroying their ability to work as a team.

We have been researching the interplay of conflict, politics, and speed in strategic decision making by top-management teams for the past ten years. In one study, we had the opportunity to observe closely the work of a dozen top-management teams in technology-based companies. All the companies competed in fast changing, competitive global markets. Thus all the teams had to make high-stakes decisions in the face of considerable uncertainty and under pressure to move quickly. Each team consisted of between five and nine executives; we were allowed to question them individually and also to observe their interactions firsthand as we tracked specific strategic decisions in the making. The study's design gives us a window on conflict as top-management teams actually experience it and highlights the role of emotion in business decision making.

In 4 of the 12 companies, there was little or no substantive disagreement over major issues and therefore little conflict to observe. But the other 8 companies experienced considerable conflict. In 4 of them, the top-management teams handled conflict in a way that avoided interpersonal hostility or discord. We've called those companies Bravo Microsystems, Premier Technologies, Star Electronics, and Triumph Computers. Executives in those companies referred to their colleagues as "smart," "team player," and "best in the business." They described the way they work as a team as "open," "fun," and "productive." The executives vigorously debated the issues, but they wasted little time on politicking and posturing. As one put it, "I really don't have time." Another said, "We don't gloss over the issues; we hit them straight on. But we're not political." Still another observed of her company's management team, "We scream a lot, then laugh, and then resolve the issue."

The other four companies in which issues were contested were less successful at avoiding interpersonal conflict. We've called those companies Andromeda Processing, Mega Software, Mercury Microdevices, and Solo Systems. Their top teams were plagued by intense animosity. Executives often failed to cooperate, rarely talking with one another,

Idea in Brief

Think "conflict" is a dirty word, especially for top-management teams? It's actually *valuable* for team members to roll up their sleeves and spar (figuratively, that is)—if they do it right. Constructive conflict helps teams make high-stakes decisions under considerable uncertainty *and* move quickly in the face of intense pressure—essential capacities in today's fast-paced markets.

The key? Mitigate *interpersonal* conflict. Most conflicts take a personal turn all too soon. Here's how your team can detach the personal from the professional—and dramatically improve its collective effectiveness.

tending to fragment into cliques, and openly displaying their frustration and anger. When executives described their colleagues to us, they used words such as "manipulative," "secretive," "burned out," and "political."

The teams with minimal interpersonal conflict were able to separate substantive issues from those based on personalities. They managed to disagree over questions of strategic significance and still get along with one another. How did they do that? After analyzing our observations of the teams' behavior, we found that their companies used the same six tactics for managing interpersonal conflict. Team members

- worked with more, rather than less, information and debated on the basis of facts;

- developed multiple alternatives to enrich the level of debate;

- shared commonly agreed-upon goals;

- injected humor into the decision process;

- maintained a balanced power structure;

- resolved issues without forcing consensus.

Those tactics were usually more implicit than explicit in the decision-making work of the management teams, and if the tactics were given names, the names varied from one organization to the next.

Idea in Practice

The best teams use these six tactics to separate substantive issues from personalities:

- **Focus on the facts.** Arm yourselves with a wealth of data about your business *and* your competitors. This encourages you to debate critical *issues*, not argue out of ignorance.

  Example: Star Electronics'* top team "measured everything": bookings, backlogs, margins, engineering milestones, cash, scrap, work-in-process. They also tracked competitors' moves, including product introductions, price changes, and ad campaigns.

- **Multiply the alternatives.** In weighing decisions, consider four or five options at once—even some you don't support. This diffuses conflict, preventing teams from polarizing around just two possibilities.

  Example: To improve Triumph Computer's* lackluster performance, managers gathered facts and then brainstormed a range of alternatives, including radically redirecting strategy with entry into a new market, and even selling the company. The team combined elements of several options to arrive at a creative, robust solution.

- **Create common goals.** Unite a team with common goals. This rallies everyone to work on decisions as collaborations, making it in *everyone's* interest to achieve the best solution.

Nonetheless, the consistency with which all four companies employed all six tactics is testimony to their effectiveness. Perhaps most surprising was the fact that the tactics did not delay—and often accelerated—the pace at which the teams were able to make decisions.

Focus on the Facts

Some managers believe that working with too much data will increase interpersonal conflict by expanding the range of issues for debate. We found that more information is better—if the data are objective and up-to-date—because it encourages people to focus on issues, not personalities. At Star Electronics, for example, the members of the top-management team typically examined a wide variety of operating

Example: Star Electronic's* rallying cry was the goal of creating *"the* computer firm of the decade." Premier Technologies' was to "build the best damn machine on the market."

- **Use humor.** Humor—even if it seems contrived at times—relieves tension and promotes collaborative esprit within a team. Practical jokes, Halloween and April Fool's Day celebrations, and "dessert pig-outs" relax everyone—increasing tactfulness, effective listening, and creativity.

- **Balance the power structure.** The CEO is more powerful than other executives, but the others wield substantial power as well—especially in their own areas of responsibility. This lets the whole team participate in strategic decisions, establishing fairness and equity.

- **Seek consensus with qualification.** If the team can't reach consensus, the most relevant senior manager makes the decision, guided by input from the others. Like balancing the power structure, this tactic also builds fairness and equity.

Example: At Premier Technologies*, managers couldn't agree on a response to a competitor's new-product launch. Ultimately, the CEO and his marketing VP madethe decision. Quipped the CEO: "The function heads do the talking; I pull the trigger."

*All company names have been changed.

measures on a monthly, weekly, and even daily basis. They claimed to "measure everything." In particular, every week they fixed their attention on indicators such as bookings, backlogs, margins, engineering milestones, cash, scrap, and work-in-process. Every month, they reviewed an even more comprehensive set of measures that gave them extensive knowledge of what was actually happening in the corporation. As one executive noted, "We have very strong controls."

Star's team also relied on facts about the external environment. One senior executive was charged with tracking such moves by competitors as product introductions, price changes, and ad campaigns. A second followed the latest technical developments through his network of contacts in universities and other companies. "We over-M.B.A. it," said the CEO, characterizing Star's zealous pursuit of data. Armed with the facts, Star's executives had an extraordinary grasp of the details of their business, allowing them to focus debate on critical issues and avoid useless arguments rooted in ignorance.

At Triumph Computer, we found a similar dedication to current facts. The first person the new CEO hired was an individual to track the progress of engineering-development projects, the new-product lifeblood of the company. Such knowledge allowed the top-management team to work from a common base of facts.

In the absence of good data, executives waste time in pointless debate over opinions. Some resort to self-aggrandizement and ill-formed guesses about how the world might be. People—and not issues—become the focus of disagreement. The result is interpersonal conflict. In such companies, top managers are often poorly informed both about internal operations, such as bookings and engineering milestones, and about external issues, such as competing products. They collect data narrowly and infrequently. In these companies, the vice presidents of finance, who oversee internal data collection, are usually weak. They were often described by people in the companies we studied as "inexperienced" or "detached." In contrast, the vice president of finance at Premier Technologies, a company with little interpersonal conflict, was described as being central to taking "the constant pulse of how the firm is doing."

Management teams troubled by interpersonal conflict rely more on hunches and guesses than on current data. When they consider facts, they are more likely to examine a past measure, such as profitability, which is both historical and highly refined. These teams favor planning based on extrapolation and intuitive attempts to predict the future, neither of which yields current or factual results. Their conversations are more subjective. The CEO of one of the four high-conflict teams told us his interest in operating numbers was "minimal," and he described his goals as "subjective." At another such company, senior managers saw the CEO as "visionary" and "a little detached from the day-to-day operations." Compare those executives with the CEO of Bravo Microsystems, who had a reputation for being a "pragmatic numbers guy."

There is a direct link between reliance on facts and low levels of interpersonal conflict. Facts let people move quickly to the central issues surrounding a strategic choice. Decision makers don't become bogged down in arguments over what the facts *might* be. More important, reliance on current data grounds strategic discussions in reality. Facts (such as current sales, market share, R&D expenses, competitors' behavior, and manufacturing yields) depersonalize the discussion because they are not someone's fantasies, guesses, or self-serving desires. In the absence of facts, individuals' motives are likely to become suspect. Building decisions on facts creates a culture that emphasizes issues instead of personalities.

Multiply the Alternatives

Some managers believe that they can reduce conflict by focusing on only one or two alternatives, thus minimizing the dimensions over which people can disagree. But, in fact, teams with low incidences of interpersonal conflict do just the opposite. They deliberately develop multiple alternatives, often considering four or five options at once. To promote debate, managers will even introduce options they do not support.

For example, Triumph's new CEO was determined to improve the company's lackluster performance. When he arrived, new products were stuck in development, and investors were getting anxious. He launched a fact-gathering exercise and asked senior executives to develop alternatives. In less than two months, they developed four. The first was to sell some of the company's technology. The second was to undertake a major strategic redirection, using the base technology to enter a new market. The third was to redeploy engineering resources and adjust the marketing approach. The final option was to sell the company.

Working together to shape those options enhanced the group's sense of teamwork while promoting a more creative view of Triumph's competitive situation and its technical competencies. As a result, the team ended up combining elements of several options in a way that was more robust than any of the options were individually.

The other teams we observed with low levels of interpersonal conflict also tended to develop multiple options to make major decisions. Star, for example, faced a cash flow crisis caused by explosive growth. Its executives considered, among other choices, arranging for lines of credit from banks, selling additional stock, and forming strategic alliances with several partners. At Bravo, managers explicitly relied on three kinds of alternatives: sincere proposals that the proponent actually backed; support for someone else's proposal, even if only for the sake of argument; and insincere alternatives proposed just to expand the number of options.

There are several reasons why considering multiple alternatives may lower interpersonal conflict. For one, it diffuses conflict: choices become less black and white, and individuals gain more room to vary the degree of their support over a range of choices. Managers can more easily shift positions without losing face.

Generating options is also a way to bring managers together in a common and inherently stimulating task. It concentrates their energy on solving problems, and it increases the likelihood of obtaining integrative solutions—alternatives that incorporate the views of a greater number of the decision makers. In generating multiple alternatives, managers do not stop at obvious solutions; rather, they continue generating further—usually more original—options. The process in itself is creative and fun, setting a positive tone for substantive, instead of interpersonal, conflict.

By contrast, in teams that vigorously debate just one or two options, conflict often does turn personal. At Solo Systems, for instance, the top-management team considered entering a new business area as a way to boost the company's performance. They debated this alternative versus the status quo but failed to consider other options. Individual executives became increasingly entrenched on one side of the debate or the other. As positions hardened, the conflict became more pointed and personal. The animosity grew so great that a major proponent of change quit the company in disgust while the rest of the team either disengaged or slipped into intense and dysfunctional politicking.

Create Common Goals

A third tactic for minimizing destructive conflict involves framing strategic choices as collaborative, rather than competitive, exercises. Elements of collaboration and competition coexist within any management team: executives share a stake in the company's performance, yet their personal ambitions may make them rivals for power. The successful groups we studied consistently framed their decisions as collaborations in which it was in everyone's interest to achieve the best possible solution for the collective.

They did so by creating a common goal around which the team could rally. Such goals do not imply homogeneous thinking, but they do require everyone to share a vision. As Steve Jobs, who is associated with three high-profile Silicon Valley companies—Apple, NeXT, and Pixar—has advised, "It's okay to spend a lot of time arguing about which route to take to San Francisco when everyone wants to end up there, but a lot of time gets wasted in such arguments if one person wants to go to San Francisco and another secretly wants to go to San Diego."

Teams hobbled by conflict lack common goals. Team members perceive themselves to be in competition with one another and, surprisingly, tend to frame decisions negatively, as reactions to threats. At Andromeda Processing, for instance, the team focused on responding to a particular instance of poor performance, and team members tried to pin the blame on one another. That negative framing contrasts with the positive approach taken by Star Electronics executives, who, sharing a common goal, viewed a cash crisis not as a threat but as an opportunity to "build the biggest war chest" for an impending competitive battle. At a broad level, Star's executives shared the goal of creating "*the* computer firm of the decade." As one Star executive told us, "We take a corporate, not a functional, viewpoint most of the time."

Likewise, all the management team members we interviewed at Premier Technologies agreed that their common goal—their rallying cry—was to build "the best damn machine on the market." Thus in their debates they could disagree about critical technical alternatives—in-house versus offshore manufacturing options, for example, or alternative distribution channels—without letting the conflict turn personal.

Many studies of group decision making and intergroup conflict demonstrate that common goals build team cohesion by stressing the shared interest of all team members in the outcome of the debate. When team members are working toward a common goal, they are less likely to see themselves as individual winners and losers and are far more likely to perceive the opinions of others correctly and to learn from them. We observed that when executives lacked common goals, they tended to be closed-minded and more likely to misinterpret and blame one another.

Use Humor

Teams that handle conflict well make explicit—and often even contrived—attempts to relieve tension and at the same time promote a collaborative esprit by making their business fun. They emphasize the excitement of fast-paced competition, not the stress of competing in brutally tough and uncertain markets.

All the teams with low interpersonal conflict described ways in which they used humor on the job. Executives at Bravo Microsystems enjoyed playing gags around the office. For example, pink plastic flamingos—souvenirs from a customer—graced Bravo's otherwise impeccably decorated headquarters. Similarly, Triumph Computers' top managers held a monthly "dessert pig-out," followed by group weight watching. Those seemingly trivial activities were part of the CEO's deliberate plan to make work more fun, despite the pressures of the industry. At Star Electronics, making the company "a fun place" was an explicit goal for the top-management team. Laughter was common during management meetings. Practical jokes were popular at Star, where executives—along with other employees—always celebrated Halloween and April Fools' Day.

At each of these companies, executives acknowledged that at least some of the attempts at humor were contrived—even forced. Even so, they helped to release tension and promote collaboration.

Humor was strikingly absent in the teams marked by high inter-personal conflict. Although pairs of individuals were sometimes friends, team members shared no group social activities beyond a standard holiday party or two, and there were no conscious attempts to create humor. Indeed, the climate in which decisions were made was often just the opposite—hostile and stressful.

Humor works as a defense mechanism to protect people from the stressful and threatening situations that commonly arise in the course of making strategic decisions. It helps people distance them-selves psychologically by putting those situations into a broader life context, often through the use of irony. Humor—with its ambiguity—can also blunt the threatening edge of negative information. Speak-ers can say in jest things that might otherwise give offense because the message is simultaneously serious and not serious. The recipient is allowed to save face by receiving the serious message while appearing not to do so. The result is communication of difficult infor-mation in a more tactful and less personally threatening way.

Humor can also move decision making into a collaborative rather than competitive frame through its powerful effect on mood. Accor-ding to a large body of research, people in a positive mood tend to be not only more optimistic but also more forgiving of others and creative in seeking solutions. A positive mood triggers a more accurate percep-tion of others' arguments because people in a good mood tend to relax their defensive barriers and so can listen more effectively.

Balance the Power Structure

We found that managers who believe that their team's decision-making process is fair are more likely to accept decisions without resentment, even when they do not agree with them. But when they believe the process is unfair, ill will easily grows into interpersonal conflict. A fifth tactic for taming interpersonal conflict, then, is to create a sense of fairness by balancing power within the manage-ment team.

Our research suggests that autocratic leaders who manage through highly centralized power structures often generate high levels of interpersonal friction. At the other extreme, weak leaders also engender interpersonal conflict because the power vacuum at the top encourages managers to jockey for position. Interpersonal conflict is lowest in what we call *balanced power structures,* those in which the CEO is more powerful than the other members of the top-management team, but the members do wield substantial power, especially in their own well-defined areas of responsibility. In balanced power structures, all executives participate in strategic decisions.

At Premier Technologies, for example, the CEO—described by others as a "team player"—was definitely the most powerful figure. But each executive was the most powerful decision maker in some clearly defined area. In addition, the entire team participated in all significant decisions. The CEO, one executive observed, "depends on picking good people and letting them operate."

The CEO of Bravo Microsystems, another company with a balanced power structure, summarized his philosophy as "making quick decisions involving as many people as possible." We watched the Bravo team over several months as it grappled with a major

How teams argue but still get along

Tactic ⟶	Strategy
Base discussion on current, factual information. Develop multiple alternatives to enrich the debate.	Focus on issues, not personalities.
Rally around goals. Inject humor into the decision-making process.	Frame decisions as collaborations aimed at achieving the best possible solution for the company.
Maintain a balanced power structure. Resolve issues without forcing consensus.	Establish a sense of fairness and equity in the process.

strategic redirection. After many group discussions, the final decision was made at a multiday retreat involving the whole team.

In contrast, the leaders of the teams marked by extensive interpersonal conflict were either highly autocratic or weak. The CEO at Mercury Microdevices, for example, was the principal decision maker. There was a substantial gap in power between him and the rest of the team. In the decision we tracked, the CEO dominated the process from start to finish, identifying the problem, defining the analysis, and making the choice. Team members described the CEO as "strong" and "dogmatic." As one of them put it, "When Bruce makes a decision, it's like God!"

At Andromeda, the CEO exercised only modest power, and areas of responsibility were blurred within the top-management team, where power was diffuse and ambiguous. Senior executives had to politick amongst themselves to get anything accomplished, and they reported intense frustration with the confusion that existed at the top.

Most executives expected to control some significant aspect of their business but not the entirety. When they lacked power—because of either an autocrat or a power vacuum—they became frustrated by their inability to make significant decisions. Instead of team members, they became politicians. As one executive explained, "We're all jockeying for our spot in the pecking order." Another described "maneuvering for the CEO's ear."

The situations we observed are consistent with classic social-psychology studies of leadership. For example, in a study from the 1960s, Ralph White and Ronald Lippitt examined the effects of different leadership styles on boys in social clubs. They found that boys with democratic leaders—the situation closest to our balanced power structure—showed spontaneous interest in their activities. The boys were highly satisfied, and within their groups there were many friendly remarks, much praise, and significant collaboration. Under weak leaders, the boys were disorganized, inefficient, and dissatisfied. But the worst case was autocratic rule, under which the boys were hostile and aggressive, occasionally directing physical violence against innocent scapegoats. In imbalanced power situations, we observed adult displays of verbal aggression that colleagues described as violent. One executive talked about being "caught in the cross fire." Another described a colleague as "a gun about to go off." A third spoke about "being beat up" by the CEO.

Seek Consensus with Qualification

Balancing power is one tactic for building a sense of fairness. Finding an appropriate way to resolve conflict over issues is another—and, perhaps, the more crucial. In our research, the teams that managed conflict effectively all used the same approach to resolving substantive conflict. It is a two-step process that some executives call *consensus with qualification*. It works like this: executives talk over an issue and try to reach consensus. If they can, the decision is made. If they can't, the most relevant senior manager makes the decision, guided by input from the rest of the group.

When a competitor launched a new product attacking Premier Technologies in its biggest market, for example, there was sharp disagreement about how to respond. Some executives wanted to shift R&D resources to counter this competitive move, even at the risk of diverting engineering talent from a more innovative product then in design. Others argued that Premier should simply repackage an existing product, adding a few novel features. A third group felt that the threat was not serious enough to warrant a major response.

After a series of meetings over several weeks, the group failed to reach consensus. So the CEO and his marketing vice president made the decision. As the CEO explained, "The functional heads do the talking. I pull the trigger." Premier's executives were comfortable with this arrangement—even those who did not agree with the outcome—because everyone had had a voice in the process.

People usually associate consensus with harmony, but we found the opposite: teams that insisted on resolving substantive conflict by forcing consensus tended to display the most interpersonal conflict. Executives sometimes have the unrealistic view that consensus is always possible, but such a naïve insistence on consensus can lead to endless haggling. As the vice president of engineering at Mega Software put it, "Consensus means that everyone has veto power. Our products were too late, and they were too expensive." At Andromeda, the CEO wanted his executives to reach consensus, but persistent differences of opinion remained. The debate dragged on for months, and the frustration mounted until some top managers simply gave up. They just wanted a decision, any decision. One was finally made when several executives who favored one point of view left the company. The price of consensus was a decimated team.

In a team that insists on consensus, deadlines can cause executives to sacrifice fairness and thus weaken the team's support for the final decision. At Andromeda, executives spent months analyzing their industry and developing a shared perspective on important trends for the future, but they could never focus on making the decision. The decision-making process dragged on. Finally, as the deadline of a board meeting drew imminent, the CEO formulated and announced a choice—one that had never even been mentioned in the earlier discussions. Not surprisingly, his team was angry and upset. Had he been less insistent on reaching a consensus, the CEO would not have felt forced by the deadline to act so arbitrarily.

How does consensus with qualification create a sense of fairness? A body of research on procedural justice shows that process fairness, which involves significant participation and influence by all concerned, is enormously important to most people. Individuals are willing to accept outcomes they dislike if they believe that the process by which those results came about was fair. Most people want their opinions to be considered seriously but are willing to accept that those opinions cannot always prevail. That is precisely what occurs in consensus with qualification. As one executive at Star said, "I'm happy just to bring up my opinions."

Apart from fairness, there are several other reasons why consensus with qualification is an important deterrent to interpersonal conflict. It assumes that conflict is natural and not a sign of interpersonal dysfunction. It gives managers added influence when the decision affects their part of the organization in particular, thus

Building a Fighting Team

HOW CAN MANAGERS ENCOURAGE the kind of substantive debate over issues that leads to better decision making? We found five approaches that help generate constructive disagreement within a team:

1. **Assemble a heterogeneous team, including diverse ages, genders, functional backgrounds, and industry experience.** If everyone in the executive meetings looks alike and sounds alike, then the chances are excellent that they probably think alike, too.

2. **Meet together as a team regularly and often.** Team members that don't know one another well don't know one another's positions on issues, impairing their ability to argue effectively. Frequent interaction builds the mutual confidence and familiarity team members require to express dissent.

3. **Encourage team members to assume roles beyond their obvious product, geographic, or functional responsibilities.** Devil's advocates, sky-gazing visionaries, and action-oriented executives can work together to ensure that all sides of an issue are considered.

4. **Apply multiple mind-sets to any issue.** Try role-playing, putting yourself in your competitors' shoes, or conducting war games. Such techniques create fresh perspectives and engage team members, spurring interest in problem solving.

5. **Actively manage conflict.** Don't let the team acquiesce too soon or too easily. Identify and treat apathy early, and don't confuse a lack of conflict with agreement. Often, what passes for consensus is really disengagement.

---

balancing managers' desires to be heard with the need to make a choice. It is an equitable and egalitarian process of decision making that encourages everyone to bring ideas to the table but clearly delineates how the decision will be made.

Finally, consensus with qualification is fast. Processes that require consensus tend to drag on endlessly, frustrating managers with what they see as time-consuming and useless debate. It's not surprising that the managers end up blaming their frustration on the shortcomings of their colleagues and not on the poor conflict-resolution process.

Linking Conflict, Speed, and Performance

A considerable body of academic research has demonstrated that conflict over issues is not only likely within top-management teams but also valuable. Such conflict provides executives with a more inclusive range of information, a deeper understanding of the issues, and a richer set of possible solutions. That was certainly the case in the companies we studied. The evidence also overwhelmingly indicates that where there is little conflict over issues, there is also likely to be poor decision making. "Groupthink" has been a primary cause of major corporate- and public-policy debacles. And although it may seem counterintuitive, we found that the teams that engaged in healthy conflict over issues not only made better decisions but moved more quickly as well. Without conflict, groups lose their effectiveness. Managers often become withdrawn and only superficially harmonious. Indeed, we found that the alternative to conflict is usually not agreement but apathy and disengagement. Teams unable to foster substantive conflict ultimately achieve, on average, lower performance. Among the companies that we observed, low-conflict teams tended to forget to consider key issues or were simply unaware of important aspects of their strategic situation. They missed opportunities to question falsely limiting assumptions or to generate significantly different alternatives. Not surprisingly, their actions were often easy for competitors to anticipate.

In fast-paced markets, successful strategic decisions are most likely to be made by teams that promote active and broad conflict over issues without sacrificing speed. The key to doing so is to mitigate interpersonal conflict.

Originally published in July 1997. Reprint 97402

About the Contributors

TERESA M. AMABILE is the Edsel Bryant Ford Professor of Business Administration at Harvard Business School.

KRISTIN BEHFAR is an assistant professor of organization and management at the University of California, Irvine.

L.J. BOURGEOIS III is a professor of business administration at the University of Virginia's Darden Graduate School of Business.

ANDY BOYNTON is the dean of Boston College's Carroll School of Management.

JEANNE BRETT is the DeWitt W. Buchanan, Jr., Distinguished Professor of Dispute Resolution and Organizations and the director of the Dispute Resolution Research Center at Northwestern University's Kellogg School of Management.

DIANE COUTU is the director of client communications at Banyan Family Business Advisors. She was formerly a senior editor at HBR.

KATHLEEN M. EISENHARDT is a professor of strategy and organization at Stanford University.

TAMARA J. ERICKSON is the CEO and founder of Tammy Erickson Associates, a firm that helps leaders build intelligent organizations.

BILL FISCHER is a professor of technology management at IMD in Lausanne, Switzerland.

BOB FRISCH is the managing partner of the Strategic Offsites Group in Boston.

LYNDA GRATTON is a professor of management practice at London Business School.

JEAN L. KAHWAJY is the founder of Effective Interactions, a communication and leadership consulting firm in Los Altos, California.

JON R. KATZENBACH is a senior partner in the New York office of Booz & Company.

MARY C. KERN is an associate professor of management at Baruch College.

STEVEN J. KRAMER is an independent researcher, writer, and consultant in Wayland, Massachusetts.

ALEX "SANDY" PENTLAND is a professor at MIT, the director of MIT's Human Dynamics Laboratory and the MIT Media Lab Entrepreneurship Program, and the chairman of Sociometric Solutions.

DOUGLAS K. SMITH is chairman of the board of The Rapid Results Institute.

VANESSA URCH DRUSKAT is an associate professor of organizational behavior and management at the University of New Hampshire and a principal at the consulting firm GEI Partners.

STEVEN B. WOLFF is a principal at the consulting firm GEI Partners.

Index

Engage with HBR content the way you want, on any device.

With HBR's new subscription plans, you can access world-renowned **case studies** from Harvard Business School and receive **four free eBooks**. Download and customize prebuilt **slide decks and graphics** from our **Visual Library**. With HBR's archive, top 50 best-selling articles, and five new articles every day, HBR is more than just a magazine.

Subscribe Today
hbr.org/success

The most important management ideas all in one place.

We hope you enjoyed this book from *Harvard Business Review*. Now you can get even more with HBR's 10 Must Reads Boxed Set. From books on leadership and strategy to managing yourself and others, this 6-book collection delivers articles on the most essential business topics to help you succeed.

HBR's 10 Must Reads Series

The definitive collection of ideas and best practices on our most sought-after topics from the best minds in business.

- Change Management
- Collaboration
- Communication
- Emotional Intelligence
- Innovation
- Leadership
- Making Smart Decisions

- Managing Across Cultures
- Managing People
- Managing Yourself
- Strategic Marketing
- Strategy
- Teams
- The Essentials

hbr.org/mustreads

Buy for your team, clients, or event.
Visit hbr.org/bulksales for quantity discount rates.